PEAK TOPO GUIDEBOOKS

Gritstone: Volume 1

STANAGE

Series Editor   **Geoff Milburn**

Volume Originator   **John Street**
assisted by
Dave Gregory

Guidebook Committee

Malc Baxter   Hilary Lawrenson
Carl Dawson   Geoff Milburn
Dave Farrant   Geoff Radcliffe
Neil Foster   Keith Sharples
Dave Gregory   Malc Taylor
Brian Griffiths   Bill Wright
Chris Hardy   Chris Wright
Graham Hoey

Produced voluntarily by the BMC Guidebook
Committee for the British Mountaineering Council

This topgraphical guidebook has been based on the 1989 Stanage guidebook. The climb numbers used in the topo refer to that host guide in which much more general information can be found.

First Topo Edition: 1993

ISBN 0 903908 96 4

Centre page photos by: Ian and Vivienne Smith

        341: Wall End Slab

        Typical Stanage Grit

        497: Left Unconquerable

Printed by:

    RAP,
    201 Spotland Road,
    Rochdale. OL12 7AF.

Distributed by:

    Cordee,
    3a De Montfort Street,
    Leicester. LE1 7HD.

BMC Peak District Guidebooks are produced on a voluntary basis and any surpluses raised are re-invested for future productions. A 5% levy is included in the price which is contributed to the BMC's Access and Conservation Fund. This is used to campaign for access to and conservation of crags and mountains throughout Britain. This is a vital contribution to climbing and its protection. The BMC would be grateful to receive other donations to support this work.

CONTENTS

Page

INTRODUCTION   4

ACKNOWLEDGEMENTS   4

THE CRAG ENVIRONMENT   5

     Access
     Parking
     Dogs
     Litter

TECHNICAL NOTES   6

     Grading of climbs
     Chipping, Bolting and Drilling
     New Routes

MOUNTAIN RESCUE   6

FIRST AID AND SAFETY ADVICE   7

USING THE TOPO   8

   Finding a climb

   Symbols used
     Climb numbers
     Crag detail

   Using location diagrams

   Access Point Diagrams   10

     Access Point No 1 Moscar Lodge
     Access Point No 2 Dennis Knoll
     Access Point No 3 Hollin Bank
     Access Point No 4 Hooks Car

THE CLIMBS   19

INDEX   135

INTRODUCTION

Since the widespread use of various forms of topo guidebook in mainland Europe and the United States the idea has gradually spread to Britain where it has been used with varying degrees of success. This topo guidebook is the first in what is planned to be a series, published by the British Mountaineering Council, covering the Peak District. The series is intended to complement rather than replace the guidebooks of traditional format. Thus with this topo guidebook to Stanage available it will be possible to leave the host guidebook at home for reading in full at leisure.

The topo is a major trial of a new approach to guidebooks and the BMC Guidebook Committee will greatly appreciate input from the climbers who use it and can comment on its acceptability and on ways to enhance the first production.

They would also welcome opinions on the overall venture, together with suggestions for future topo volumes, or even the future direction of the traditional guidebook series. Perhaps the time is ripe for a radical rethink to take guidebooks into the 21st century.

ACKNOWLEDGEMENTS

This topo guide is based on the 1989 Stanage guide and thus, like its host, relies heavily on all the preceding guidebooks which have featured Stanage. Nevertheless, a quick comparison with its predecessors will show how much it differs in material and overall approach. It has been designed by John Street with the help of Dave Gregory. New route information has come from Chris Hardy, Chris Craggs and others. Bruce Goodwin and Dave Gregory have given much support in both the concept and help in the field. Dave Farrant of the Guidebook Committee has contributed his usual expert desk top job. The strip diagrams used in the text for locational purposes are the work of George Bridge. Ian and Vivienne Smith provided the photographs.

Only the minimum technical information has been reproduced from the host guidebook which has much further detail.

CRAG ENVIRONMENT

Access

The whole of Stanage lies within the Peak District National Park. The Northern section is owned by Mr J Archdale who allows climbers on the crag providing that they observe the Country Code. They are asked to keep near the rocks and in particular not to wander on to the moor between the Stanage and Bamford Edges and not to use this section of the Edge on days when shooting is taking place. The southern section from Hooks Car (the popular end) to the iron fence by the 'Roman Road' near Enclosure Buttress is owned by the Peak Park Planning Board so that the public has freedom of access. Climbers should remember that in the northern section: THE INCLUSION OF A CRAG OR THE ROUTES UPON IT IN THIS GUIDEBOOK DOES NOT MEAN THAT ANY MEMBER OF THE PUBLIC HAS THE RIGHT OF ACCESS TO THE CRAG OR THE RIGHT TO CLIMB UPON IT.

Parking

Four Access Points with parking areas are indicated on the location diagrams. Inconsiderate parking elsewhere is a constant irritation to local landowners, farmers and rescue vehicles. Try not to block access into any fields or property.

Dogs

Dogs are a hazard to livestock, sheep in particular, and to moorland birds in the nesting season. They should always be kept on a lead. DURING THE LAMBING SEASON PLEASE LEAVE THEM AT HOME.

Litter

Please take it home along with any that you find.

TECHNICAL NOTES

Grading of climbs

For the theory governing grading of climbs refer to the host guidebook or any Saturday night discussion in a pub which climbers frequent.

Chipping, Bolting and Drilling

The national consensus is that no bolts should be placed on natural gritstone. NO BOLTING, DRILLING, or CHIPPING SHOULD TAKE PLACE ON STANAGE.

New Routes

There are some 200 newly recorded routes in this guidebook. Recording is best done by photo-copying the relevant page of the topo, marking the new line on it and sending it to Geoff Milburn, 25 Cliffe Rd, Whitfield, Glossop, Derbys. SK13 8NY with the suggested route name, grading and the names of the first ascensionists. He would be grateful if claims of solo or unseconded first ascents were accompanied by the names of witnesses.

MOUNTAIN RESCUE

Dial 999 or Ripley (0773) 43551 and ask for POLICE OPERATIONS ROOM.

Telephone kiosks are located at:

O.S. reference	Location
SK 235833	North Lees Campsite
SK 291837	Norfolk Arms Pub
SK 241807	Hathersage
SK 267803	Fox House

Rescue equipment is kept at:

1.   The Mountain Rescue Post at Hollin Bank below Stanage (SK 238836) near Access Point No 3.

2.   The Ranger Briefing Centre at Brunts Barn, Nether Padley (SK 247789). This is open from 09.00 to 17.00 hours and can be telephoned on (0433) 31405.

FIRST AID

1.   IF SPINAL INJURIES OR HEAD INJURIES are suspected, DO NOT MOVE THE PATIENT without skilled help, except to maintain breathing.

2.   IF BREATHING HAS STOPPED, clear airways and commence artificial respiration. DO NOT STOP UNTIL EXPERT OPINION DIAGNOSES DEATH.

3.   STOP BLEEDING BY APPLYING DIRECT PRESSURE AND NOT A TOURNIQUET.

4.   KEEP THE PATIENT WARM

5.   SUMMON HELP.

Reports of accidents should be sent to the Secretary of the Mountain Rescue Committee, F.J. Davies, 18 Tarnside Fold, Simmondley, Glossop, Derbyshire.

SAFETY ADVICE

Climbing is a serious pastime and can damage your health. The grades in this guidebook are given in good faith having been compiled from accounts of first ascents or past descriptions, checked and substantiated where possible, with consensus comments. Unfortunately climbs can change; rock becomes dirty, holds become worn, loose or fall off. At the time of writing there is no in situ gear on Stanage but jammed gear may not be completely safe, or may deteriorate. Even minor alterations can have a dramatic effect on the grade of a route and it is essential that climbers judge the conditions of any route before committing themselves.

The contents of this guidebook are believed to be correct; however, neither the BMC nor its members and friends involved with its production can be held responsible for any omissions or mistakes, nor be liable for any personal or third party injuries or damage, howsoever caused, arising from its use.

In our claims-conscious society climbers are recommended to obtain suitable insurance cover. The BMC provides third party liability cover for members and members of affiliated clubs.

USING THE TOPO

Finding a climb

Stanage is a 4 km long edge of possibly the finest gritstone in Britain. Finding climbs on such an extensive edge has never been easy for a first time visitor. On the rear cover is an approach map to the **four main access points for motorists**. Once there, use the appropriate **location diagram** to review the description of the key points that are easily found and the range of climbs accessible from them. At the key point use the location diagram and the crag diagrams to reach your chosen buttress.

At the foot of some of the pages is a strip diagram, drawn to a smaller scale, which has been copied from the host guide. These strips show several buttresses around the one detailed on that page and may be useful to people approaching the edge in locating where they are. The symbol * appears on the location diagrams opposite those buttresses which appear on such strip diagrams. With familiarity and good visibility you will soon take many short cuts.

For the visitor with no prior information the climbs have been grouped into areas with a name that indicates one part of the area that, by tradition, has become popular with climbers. If the richness of choice is confusing go to access point No 4 and sample the climbs between 517 – 799 at the 'popular end'. If it looks crowded go to access point No 2 and try the climbs between 147 – 194 the High Neb area.

Symbols used

Climb Numbers

The rock climbs are numbered from left to right, but since the numbers follow those of the host guide, some buttresses such as Crow Chin and a number of individual climbs with variations transgress this principle.

Where a number has a decimal point it is a new route done since the publication of the host guide or a route that was embedded in the text of the host guide with no number.

Crag Detail

Routes are shown by dotted lines: all climb details are on the same page as the diagram.

Traverses are shown by black dots and the start position is shown by a lollipop symbol above the climb number.

In the areas where descent lines are not self-evident they are shown by a black arrow head immediately above the descent point and are listed in the text where this is helpful.

Using location diagrams

From the four access points distances and directions are given to easy points to locate on the crags. The topo is laid out to give the climber a reasonable distance to walk from these points (left or right) to the chosen area.

All climbs are shown on the diagrams and the distance from each buttress to the next is shown, in square brackets, as a number of paces. If no arrow is associated with the brackets you walk horizontally. By using the major points of the compass an arrow outside the brackets indicates if you ascend or descend. If scrambling is needed this is indicated.

When there is no bracketed pace number between drawings the crag is continuous and you are simply moving to a new viewpoint of the next part. For ease of composing the pages the diagram of the next part may be offset above or below the previous one.

It is usually best to get opposite the crag by first walking an approximate distance then looking at the diagram: oblique views are often very misleading.

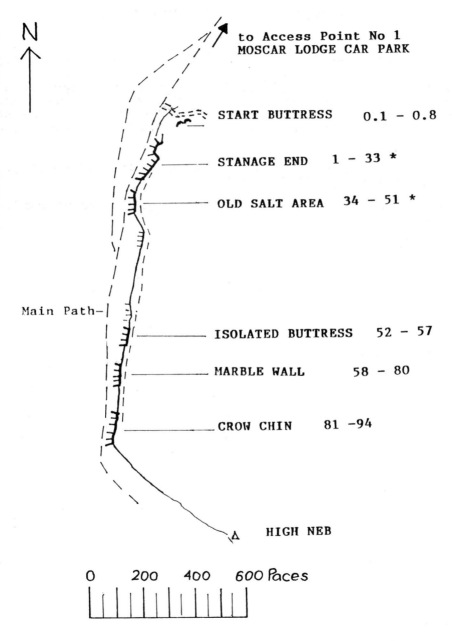

N

to Access Point No 1
MOSCAR LODGE CAR PARK

START BUTTRESS   0.1 - 0.8

STANAGE END   1 - 33 *

OLD SALT AREA   34 - 51 *

Main Path—

ISOLATED BUTTRESS   52 - 57

MARBLE WALL   58 - 80

CROW CHIN   81 -94

HIGH NEB

0   200   400   600 Paces

LOCATION DIAGRAM FOR CLIMBS :   0.1 - 94

ACCESS POINT 1: TO CLIMBS 0.1 – 94

MOSCAR LODGE CAR PARK   O.S. ref. SK 231 879

From the car park on the south side of the A57 at Moscar Lodge take the footpath south to a stile. Ascend to the moor rising gently for 1200 m until the path is joined by a wall on the left hand side. Keep the wall on the left and walk on the level for 50 paces until you reach an old quarry track on the left.

(If you turn left into the quarry and scramble out of it to the right you arrive at Start Buttress and **climb 0.1**.)

Straight ahead in 140 paces you arrive at Stanage End and **climb 0.9**.

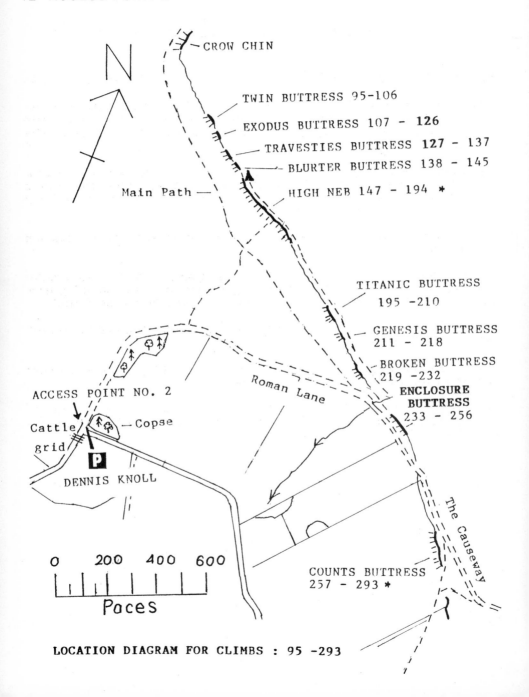

CROW CHIN

TWIN BUTTRESS 95-106

EXODUS BUTTRESS 107 - **126**

TRAVESTIES BUTTRESS **127** - 137

BLURTER BUTTRESS 138 - 145

HIGH NEB 147 - 194 *

Main Path

TITANIC BUTTRESS
195 -210

GENESIS BUTTRESS
211 - 218

BROKEN BUTTRESS
219 -232

**ENCLOSURE
BUTTRESS**
233 - 256

ACCESS POINT NO. 2

Roman Lane

Cattle
grid

Copse

DENNIS KNOLL

The Causeway

0   200   400   600

Paces

COUNTS BUTTRESS
257 - 293 *

LOCATION DIAGRAM FOR CLIMBS : 95 -293

ACCESS POINT 2: TO CLIMBS 95 – 293

DENNIS KNOLL (CATTLE GRID) CAR PARK   O.S. ref. SK 227 844

From the car park a major track 'the Roman Lane', leads north starting near a copse of young trees. Follow the track which swings right with another plantation to the right. At the end of this plantation look out for a stile on the left of the track.

(If you take the stile the path goes uphill, crossing the main path below the edge, to arrive at **climb 168** on High Neb. From here you have access leftwards as far as **climb 95** and rightwards to **195 i.e. from Twin Buttress Area to Titanic Buttress Area**).

Continue along the Roman Lane which goes east and approaches the Stanage edge.

(Close to the edge the main path will be seen going off N.W., over a stile, following the line of the crags and giving access to all the climbing from **232 to 95 i.e. from Broken Buttress Area to Twin Buttress Area**.)

On the Roman Lane you soon arrive at a wall and stream and on the left is Enclosure Buttress.

(From this point you have access to climbs **233-293 i.e. from Enclosure Buttress Area to Count's Buttress Area**.)

Note that after climb 256 the Lane rises to the top of Stanage Edge as 'the Causeway' and you must drop down to the right to locate the subsequent climbs.

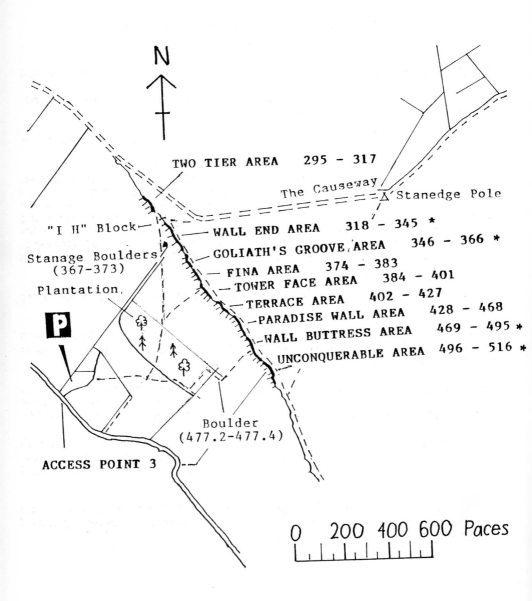

N

TWO TIER AREA   295 – 317

The Causeway

Stanedge Pole

"I H" Block

WALL END AREA   318 – 345 *

GOLIATH'S GROOVE AREA   346 – 366 *

Stanage Boulders
(367-373)

FINA AREA   374 – 383

TOWER FACE AREA   384 – 401

Plantation

TERRACE AREA   402 – 427

PARADISE WALL AREA   428 – 468

P

WALL BUTTRESS AREA   469 – 495 *

UNCONQUERABLE AREA   496 – 516 *

Boulder
(477.2-477.4)

ACCESS POINT 3

0   200 400 600 Paces

LOCATION DIAGRAM FOR CLIMBS 294.1 – 516

ACCESS POINT 3: TO CLIMBS 294.1 – 516

HOLLIN BANK (PLANTATION) CAR PARK   O.S. ref. SK 237 838

From the top of the car park a major path goes diagonally right towards the right edge of a plantation of trees.

Half way to the plantation the path swings left to become paved steps and pathway into the plantation.

(At this point a path goes right towards the right edge of the plantation. It enters the plantation and turns right along the line of an old wall. 40 paces before the end of the plantation turn left uphill and walk in the wood up to the upper boundary. Look right to a gap through the wall and a path leading to a huge boulder with **climbs 477.2-477.4**. From the far side of the boulder take the path directly uphill to reach **487 Calvary**. From here you can move leftwards as far as **428 Paradise Wall Area** and rightwards to **516 Unconquerable Area**.)

The main path enters the plantation via a gate and exits at another to continue up left.

(At the second gate an indistinct path makes directly towards Tower Face – **climb 389**. You can then go left to **346 Goliath's Groove Area** and right to **427 Terrace Area**.)

Continue up the main path to arrive at gateposts and a curving dry stone wall. (The gate posts are the starting point for climbing on the main Stanage Boulders which are immediately to your right **(climbs 367-373)**.

Continue up the flagged path to arrive at a large block on the right with 'IH' carved at knee-height. You are 40 paces below the summit edge. From the 'IH' block you reach **climbs 295 Two Tier Area-345 Wall End Area**.

(Up to the right is **climb 318 Introvert. Climb 317 Waffti** is well to the left and to reach it go up the path 40 paces to where it swings right and then go 25 paces to the left below the scarp.)

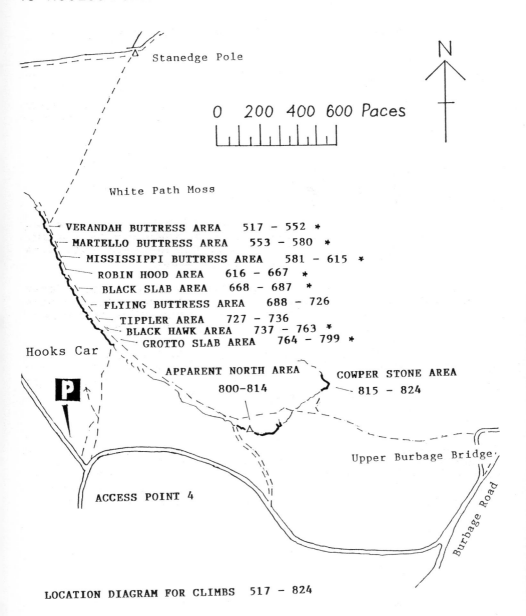

Stanedge Pole

0   200 400 600 Paces

N

White Path Moss

VERANDAH BUTTRESS AREA   517 – 552 *
MARTELLO BUTTRESS AREA   553 – 580 *
MISSISSIPPI BUTTRESS AREA   581 – 615 *
ROBIN HOOD AREA   616 – 667 *
BLACK SLAB AREA   668 – 687 *
FLYING BUTTRESS AREA   688 – 726
TIPPLER AREA   727 – 736
BLACK HAWK AREA   737 – 763 *
GROTTO SLAB AREA   764 – 799 *

Hooks Car

P

APPARENT NORTH AREA   800–814

COWPER STONE AREA   815 – 824

Upper Burbage Bridge

ACCESS POINT 4

Burbage Road

LOCATION DIAGRAM FOR CLIMBS   517 – 824

ACCESS POINT 4: TO CLIMBS 517 – 824

HOOKS CAR (POPULAR END) CAR PARK   O.S. ref. SK 244 830

There is extensive roadside parking at this access point. Set off towards the crags on a wide earth path. Keep to the upper path at the first apparent junction (150 paces).

(The lower path gives more direct access to **climb 701 Flying Buttress Area and beyond to 517.**)

At the next junction take the left branch.

(The right branch goes directly to **799 Grotto Slab Area.** There you can turn right and follow the path along the top of Stanage Edge to a trig. point. Directly below the trig. point is **climb 806 Apparent North Area** and access to **climbs 800-814 Cowper Stone Area.**)

Continue upwards to arrive at the crag where a prominent mass of fallen rock forms **Grotto Slab 766.** From this point you have access to climbs **517-799.** There are no major breaks in this magnificent escarpment and you must identify the buttresses sequentially in either direction.

From the Hooks Car access point to climb on **800-814 Apparent North Area** it is better to approach by walking up the Burbage road for 400 m and take a major path on the left-hand side which passes through gate posts. Walk up to Stanage Edge and **climb 800** is immediately on your right.

The final climbs on Stanage Edge are around the Cowper Stone and Chippy Buttress behind it. Continue to walk (or drive) up Burbage Road to Upper Burbage Bridge where there is car parking by the road side. At the bend in the road (SK 259 830) a major path crosses the heather moor towards the last section of Stanage Edge. Follow the path to the foot of the edge then cut off to the right to the Cowper Stone for **climbs 815-824.**

APPROACH FROM LODGE MOOR

The 51 bus route from Sheffield has its terminus at Lodge Moor (by the hospital) and occasionally at Wyming Brook. The metalled road continues from either terminus to end at the head of the Redmires Dams (SK 256851). A wide, unmetalled track, which has occasional single track flagged sections, then runs south-west for about 1 km to Stanedge Pole (SK 247844).

From Stanedge Pole

either:

Follow the track, which now has a short length of flagged double-track, WSW. As it nears the edge, after about half a km, it curves to the right (at SK 241844). A path runs straight ahead past a stone gate-post.

Just beyond the gate-post a left fork goes direct to the edge in fifty paces. **The Coign (349 Goliath's Groove Area)** is on the left and **Wall End Slab (341)** is on the right (both facing out).

The right fork from the gate-post swings right along the edge then back left over the crest of the edge to become a flagged path which runs down to The Plantation. **The Introvert (318)** is then the first route on the left.

The main path continues along the top of the edge, then drops obliquely down running north-west, as 'the Causeway', under **Motor Mile (256)** and **Centurion's Slab (253)** which are on the right.)

or:

If the ground is dry, an alternative is to take the track south-west across the moor past the beam bearing the notice banning vehicles and bikes. The track wanders to avoid boggy patches, and hits the edge near **Verandah Buttress (546)**.

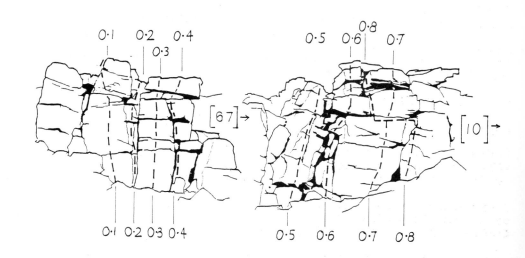

START BUTTRESS

0.1	**Start**	7m	VS	5a
0.2	**Move**	6m	HD	
0.3	**Faster**	6m	VS	5a
0.4	**Slow Down**	7m	S	
0.5	**Bath Oil**	6m	HS	
0.6	**Me**	6m	HVS	5a
0.7	**Bathtime for Two**	6m	HS	4c
0.8	**You**	8m	VS	4c

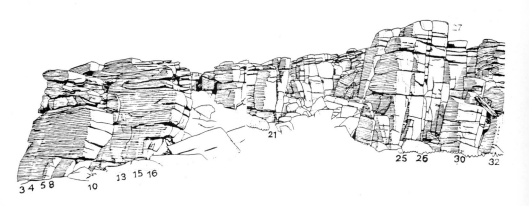

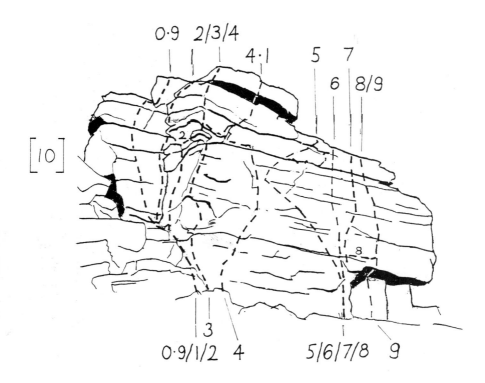

STANAGE END

0.9	Green Party	8m	VS	5a	
1	The Rack	11m	D		
2	Bad Do	9m	HVS	5a	
3	Another Turn	11m	S		
4	The Pinion	14m	VD	-	*
4.1	Steamin'	-	HVS	5a	
5	The Ariel	14m	VD	-	*
6	The Green Streak	12m	HVS	4c	**
7	Slight Second	12m	E1	5b	
8	Incursion	13m	E1	5b	*
9	Incursion Direct	12m	E1	6a	*

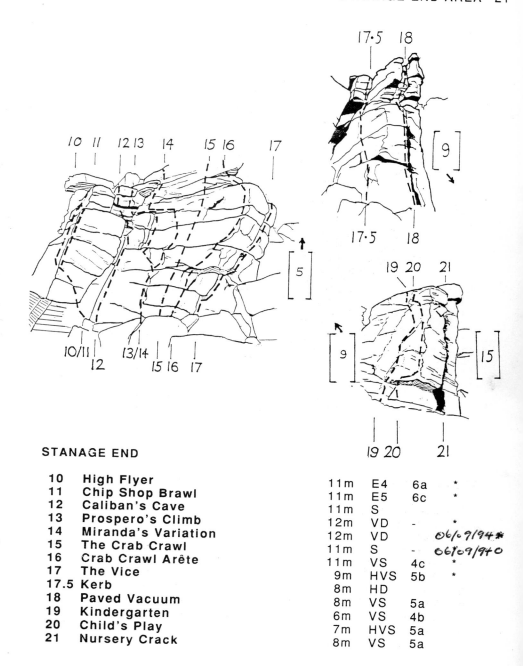

STANAGE END

10	High Flyer	11m	E4	6a	*	
11	Chip Shop Brawl	11m	E5	6c	*	
12	Caliban's Cave	11m	S			
13	Prospero's Climb	12m	VD	-	*	
14	Miranda's Variation	12m	VD		06/09/94 *	
15	The Crab Crawl	11m	S	-	06/09/94 0	
16	Crab Crawl Arête	11m	VS	4c	*	
17	The Vice	9m	HVS	5b	*	
17.5	Kerb	8m	HD			
18	Paved Vacuum	8m	VS	5a		
19	Kindergarten	6m	VS	4b		
20	Child's Play	7m	HVS	5a		
21	Nursery Crack	8m	VS	5a		

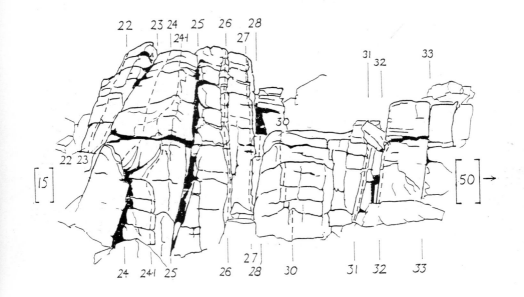

22	Doctored	12m	HVS	5c	
23	Cripple's Crack	13m	HVD		
24	Physician's Wall	13m	E1	5b	
24.1	Which Doctor?	18m	E5	6a	*
25	Doctor's Chimney	18m	VD	-	*
26	Surgeon's Saunter	18m	HVS	5b	**
27	Heath Robinson	16m	E5	6b	*
28	Niche Climb	9m	S		
29	Niche Wall (not identified)	9m	VS	5a	
30	Manhattan Arête	6m	D		
31	Manhattan Chimney	6m	D		
32	New York, New York	6m	E1	6a	
33	Manhattan Crack	6m	VS	4b	

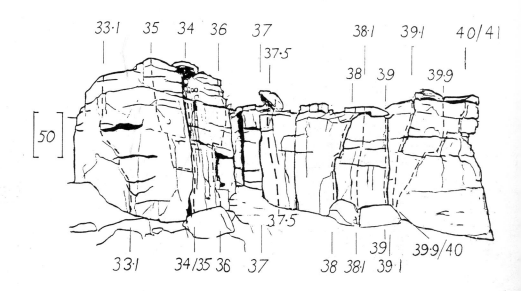

OLD SALT

33.1	Concept of Kinky	9m	E5	6c	*	
34	The Wobbler	9m	HVS	5b	*	
35	Good Clean Fun	9m	E4	6b	*	
36	Gameo	8m	E2	5b		
37	Avril	6m	S	-	*06/09/94 0*	
37.5	Mai	6m	VS	4b		
38	Mars	6m	VD			
38.1	7% Soln	6m	HVS	5b		
39	February Crack	6m	HS	4b	*	
39.1	Acute Amnesia	7m	HVS	5b		
39.9	Exaltation	8m	E5	6c	**	
40	Saltation	8m	E4	6c	*	
41	Old Salt	10m	HVS	5a	**	

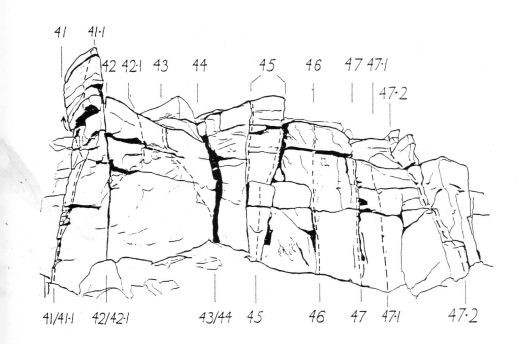

OLD SALT

41	Old Salt	10m	HVS	5a	**
41.1	Rimmington Place	-	E2	5c	
42	Valediction	9m	HVS	5a	*
42.1	The Water Seller	8m	E4	6a	
43	Monad	6m	E1	6a	
44	Boomerang Chimney	6m	VD		
45	Twin Cracks	6m	VD		
46	Quiver	6m	HVS	5c	
47	Arrow Crack	6m	VS	5a	
47.1	Blinkers	6m	VS	5a	
47.2	Balance	6m	D		

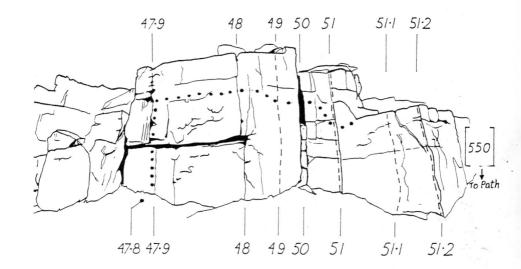

47.8	Vaccine Traverse	?m	E1	5b	
47.9	Problem Crack	6m	-	5a	
48	Microbe	6m	HVS	5c	*
49	Germ	6m	E2	6a	*
50	Crumbling Crack	6m	HS	4b	
51	Problem Corner	5m	VS	5b	
51.1	Love Handles	5m	HVS	5c	
51.2	Mr M'Quod and the Anti-rock Squad	5m	HVS	5c	

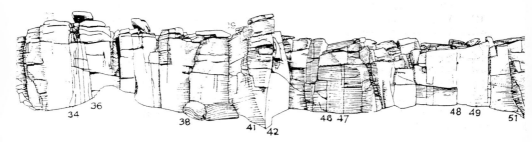

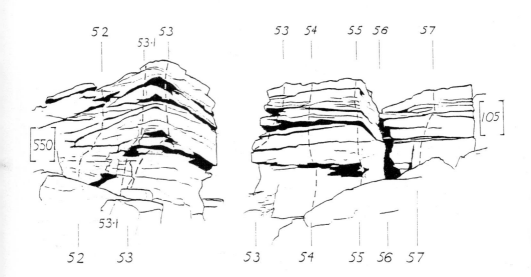

ISOLATED BUTTRESS

52	Wetness Wall	7m	D	
53	Missing Link	9m	E2	5c
53.1	Brittle Bones	8m	E1	5c
54	Clubbing	8m	E3	6b
55	Mr Pemphigoid	7m	HVS	5c
56	Lonely Crag	9m	D	
57	Flesh and Blood	6m	VS	5b

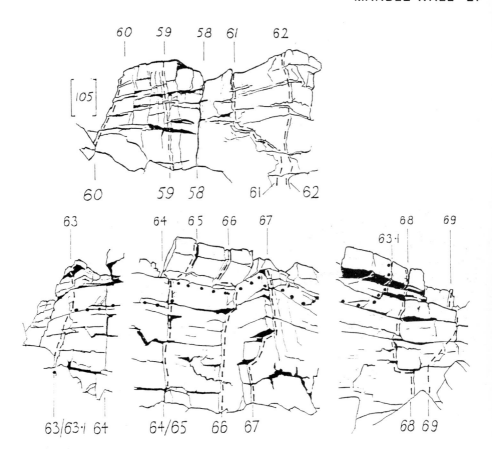

MARBLE WALL

58	Green Crack	9m	VD		
59	Spock Out	9m	VS	5a	
60	Bifurcated Headplate Max	9m	VS	4c	
61	Marble Tower Flake	11m	VD		
62	Marble Arête	11m	HS	4a	*
63	Sceptic	11m	HVS	5b	*
63.1	The Lamia (traverse)	27m	E2	5c	**
64	Terrazza Crack	11m	HVS	5b	***
65	Harvest	4m	E3	6b	**
66	Nectar	15m	E4	6b	***
67	Orang-outang	11m	E1	5c	**
68	Goosey Goosey Gander	11m	E4	6a	***
69	Don's Delight	7m	HVS	5b	

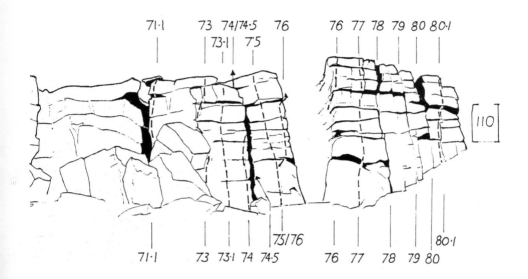

CLEFT BUTTRESS

70	**Back Door** (not identified)	10m	VS	4c
71	**Green Line** (not identified)	8m	HVS	5b
71.1	**In a Big Way Yerself**	9m	E4	6b	*
73	**Left Hand Tower**	11m	VS	4c
73.1	**Turtle Power**	11m	E6	6c	***
74	**Slap 'n' Spittle**	13m	E4	6a	*
74.5	**Pacemaker** (bridge)	15m	HVS	5b
75	**Vena Cave-in**	16m	E3	5c	*
76	**Right Hand Tower**	16m	HVS	5a	**
77	**Tempskya**	12m	E3	5c
78	**First Sister**	12m	VS	4c
79	**Second Sister**	10m	VS	4c
80	**Richard's Sister**	8m	S	
80.1	**Not Richard's Sister Direct**	8m	E1	6a

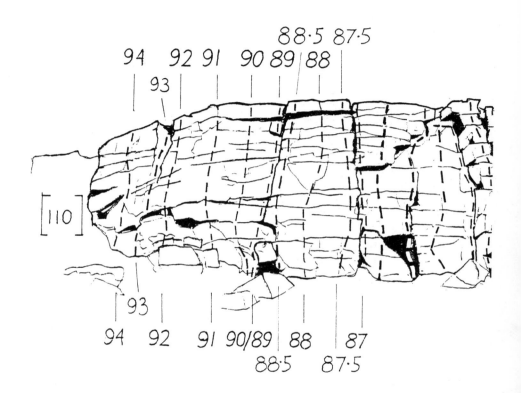

CROW CHIN (numbers on this crag run right to left)

87.5	Spring Sunshine	10m	VS	4c	
88	Kelly's Eliminate	10m	D		*
88.5	Kelly's Eye	10m	S		
89	Kelly's Crack	10m	D		
90	Feathered Friends	10m	VS	4b	
91	Perforation	9m	HVS	4c	
92	Jim Crow	9m	VS	4c	
93	Rabbit's Crack	8m	VS	4b	
94	So Many Classics, So Little Time	7m	HVS	5c	*

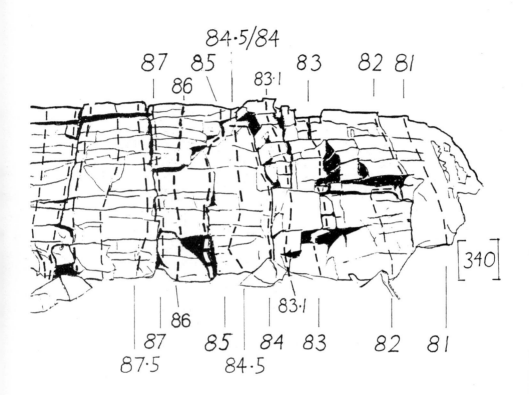

CROW CHIN (numbers on this crag run right to left)

81	**Bright Eyed**	9m	VS	4b
82	**Autumn Gold**	10m	HS	
83	**The Marmoset**	6m	HS	4c
83.1	**New Year's Eve**	10m	S	
84	**Bent Crack**	10m	HD	
84.5	**Big Al**	10m	HVS	5a
85	**October Slab**	10m	S	
86	**May Crack**	10m	VS	5a
87	**October Crack**	10m	D	

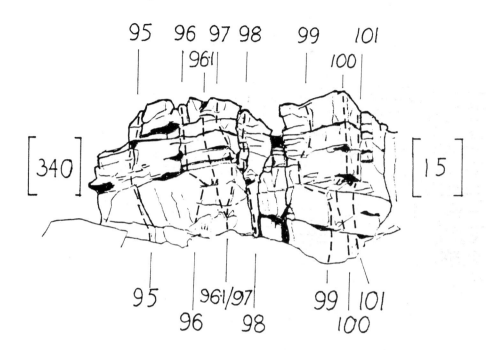

TWIN BUTTRESS

95	Undercut Crack	7m	VS	5a	
96	Bottomless Crack	8m	HVS	6a	
96.1	Lysteria Hysteria	9m	E3	6a	
97	Certainly Parakeratosis	8m	HVS	5a	
98	Bow Crack	7m	HD	-	*
99	Seranata	7m	E1	5b	*
100	Hardly Hyperkeratosis	7m	E2	5c	
101	Quadrille	6m	S	-	*

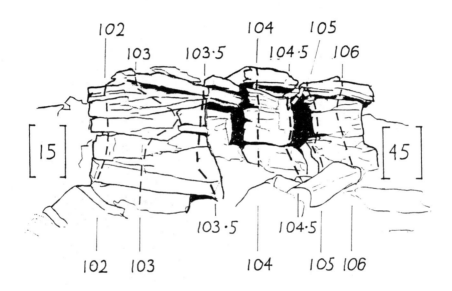

BANDIT BUTTRESS

102	Ventured Point	9m	HS	
103	Meson	9m	VD	
103.5	Lepton	8m	HS	
104	Bandits in the Woods	8m	VS	5a
104.5	Spectacle	8m	S	
105	Side Effect	9m	VS	4c
106	Thalidomide	8m	E2	5c

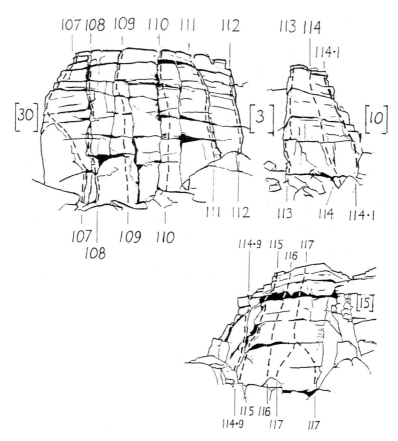

EXODUS BUTTRESS

107	Cheeky Little Number	9m	E1	5b	
108	Exodus	10m	HVS	5a	*
109	Deuteronomy	1m	HVS	5b	**
110	Leviticus	10m	HVS	5b	*
111	Missing Numbers	10m	HVS	5b	
112	E.M.F.	7m	VS	4c	
113	Treatment	6m	VS	5a	
114	Sudoxe	8m	HVS	5a	*
114.1	Radox	7m	S		
114.9	Jam Good	8m	VD		
115	Pup	8m	HVS	6a	
116	Puss	8m	HVS	5c	
117	Kitten	8m	VS	5b	

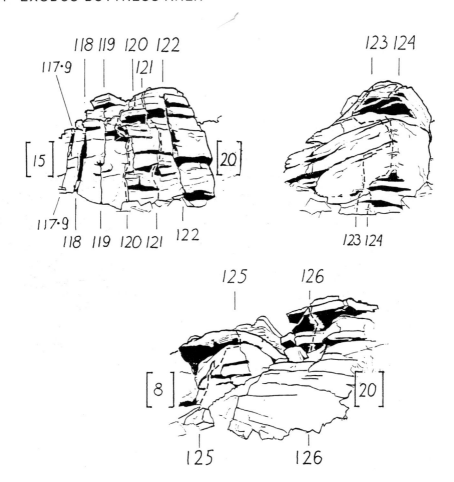

COSMIC BUTTRESS

117.9	Pulse	6m	HVS	5a	
118	Beanpod	6m	S		
119	X-ray	7m	HS		
120	Electron	8m	VS	4c	
121	Quantum Crack	9m	VS	5a	
122	Cosmic Crack	9m	VS	4c	**
123	Birthday Buttress	10m	HS	4b	
124	21 Today	7m	HVS	5c	
125	Life Begins at 40	6m	HVS	5a	
126	Little Things	4m	VS	6a	

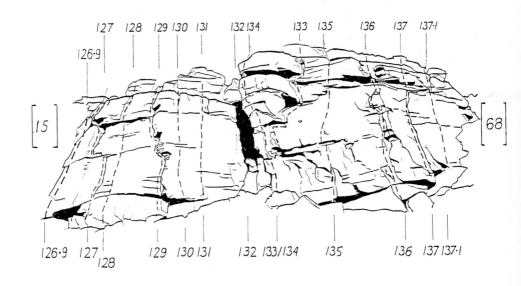

TRAVESTIES BUTTRESS

126.9	Erica Micra	5m	HS		*21/09/94 ✱ 6*	
127	Heather Crack	6m	HVD			
128	Flipside	6m	E2	5c		
129	Travesties	7m	HVS	5b	*	
130	Timothy Twinkletoes	7m	E3	6b		
131	Pig's Ear	6m	E1	6a	*	
132	Deep Chimney	7m	D			
133	Crew Pegs Diffs	8m	E3	6a	*	
134	Suitored	8m	E4	6a		
135	No More Excuses	8m	E4	6b	***	
136	The Knutter	9m	HVS	5b	*	
137	Hearsay Crack	9m	HVS	5a	*	
137.1	Pure Gossip	9m	HS	4b		

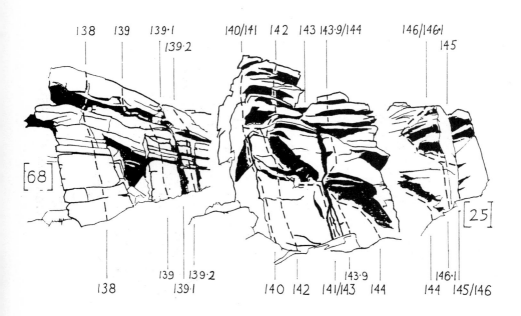

BLURTER BUTTRESS

138	Overcoat	12m	HVS	5b	
139	Lucy's Slab	12m	HVS	5b	
139.1	Stairway Crack	-	Easy		
139.2	Jean's Route	12m	VS	4c	
140	Meddle	18m	E2	5c	
141	The Blurter	21m	HVS	5b	**
142	Youth Meat	18m	E4	6b	
143	Overhanging Chimney	16m	VD		
143.9	Wolf Solent Variant	16m	E4	6a	
144	Wolf Solent	16m	E4	5c	**
145	Aries	10m	S		*
146	Typhoon	12m	HS		
146.1	Typhoon Direct	12m	E3	6a	

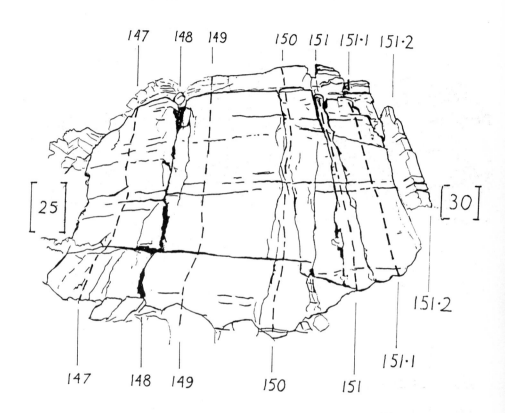

FATE BUTTRESS

147	Ono	8m	S	-	*
148	Uno Crack	9m	D		
149	Fate	9m	HVS	5c	*
150	Rinty	9m	VS	5a	
151	Duo Crack Climb	9m	D	21/09/94✱G	
151.1	Solo Slab	9m	HVS	5a	
151.2	Staircase Rib	9m	MD		

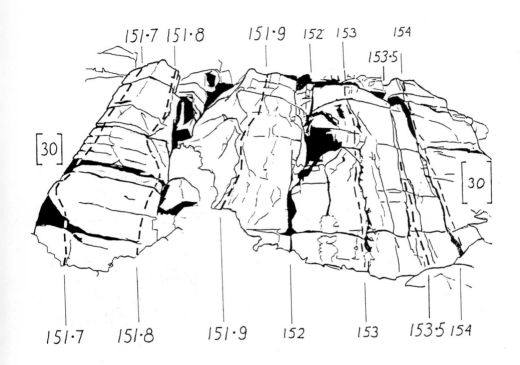

FROSTY BUTTRESS

151.7 Side Plate	8m	S	
151.8 Ice Cream Flakes	8m	VD	
151.9 Warm Afternoon	9m	VD	
152 Frosty	9m	D	
153 Icy Crack	9m	VS	4c
153.5 Freeze	9m	HVS	5b
154 Youth	8m	VD	

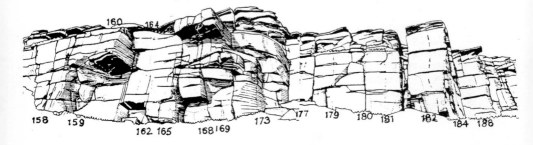

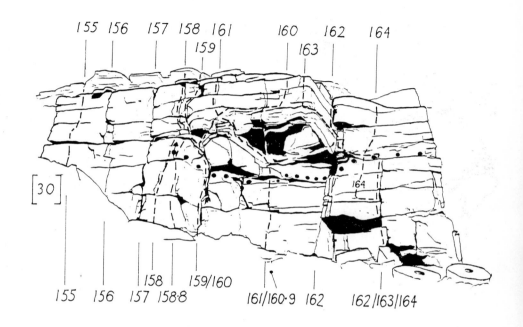

HIGH NEB

155	Way Fruitsome Experience	5m	HVS	5c	
156	Gunter	12m	VS	4c	
157	Straight Crack	14m	S	4a	
158	Eric's Eliminate	14m	S	-	*
158.8	Twisting Crack Direct	14m	-	5b	
159	Twisting Crack	14m	S	-	*
160	Kelly's Overhang	15m	HVS	5b	**
160.9	Inaccessible Slab (traverse)	-	S		
161	Mouthpiece	15m	E2	5c	
162	Inaccessible Crack	18m	VS	4c	*
163	Overflow	20m	E1	5b	
164	The Beautician	16m	E3	5c	*

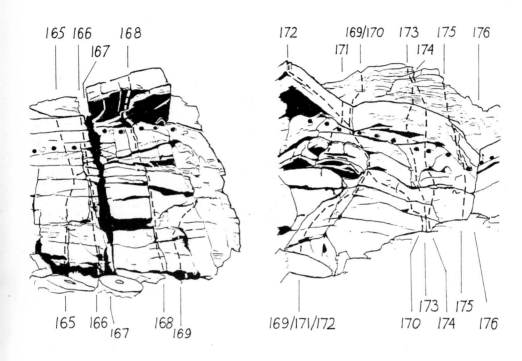

HIGH NEB

165	Impossible Slab	14m	E2	5c	**
166	Eckhard's Arête	12m	S		
167	Eckhard's Chimney	12m	VD		
168	Quietus	14m	E2	5c	***
169	Norse Corner Climb	14m	HS	4c	*
170	Kelly's Variation	6m	VD		
171	Silence	14m	HVS	5b	
172	Quietus Right-hand	12m	E4	6a	*
173	King Kong	12m	E3	6a	*
174	The Logic Book	11m	E2	5c	*
175	Sogines	11m	HVS	5a	
176	Neb Corner	11m	D		

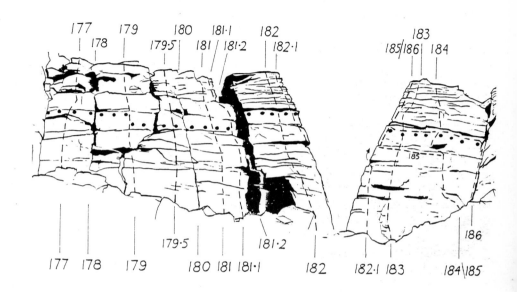

HIGH NEB

177	Cent	12m	E1	5b	
178	Boyd's Crack	12m	M		
179	Limbo	12m	S		
179.5	Lost Soul	12m	S		
180	Tango Crack	12m	VD	*21/09/94* 6.	
181	Tango Buttress	12m	HS	5a	*
181.1	Where did my Tango?	12m	VS	5a	
181.2	High Neb Gully	-	-		
182	High Neb Buttress	12m	VS	4c	***
182.1	High Neb Edge	12m	HVS	5b	
183	The Crypt Trip	19m	E5	6b	***
184	Old Friends	19m	E4	5c	***
185	The Modest Carpenter	19m	E4	6b	
186	The Dalesman	19m	HVS	5a	

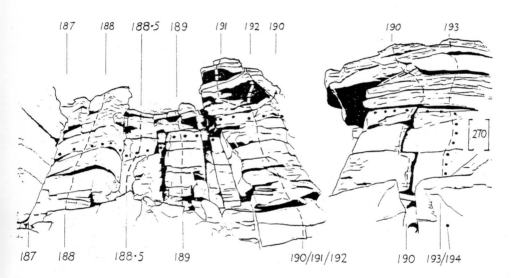

HIGH NEB

187	**Ami**	14m	M		
188	**Mantelshelf Climb**	14m	D		
188.5	**Little Slab**	14m	D		
189	**Typical Grit**	6m	VD		
190	**Cave Buttress**	15m	VD		
191	**High and Wild**	15m	E3	5c	*
192	**Jeepers Creepers**	15m	HVS	5b	*
193	**Teenage Lobotomy**	9m	HVS	5a	
194	**High Neb Girdle Traverse**	90m	S		**

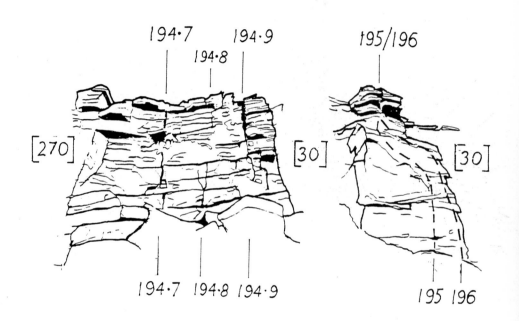

HEATHER SLAB

194.7 Calluna
194.8 Erica
194.9 Daboecia
195   Clegg
196   Midge

CLEG SLAB

10m	M	-	*
10m	M		
10m	M		
8m	HVD		
12m	D		

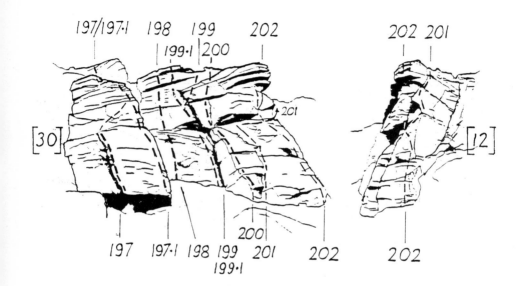

TITANIC BUTTRESS

197	**Gnat's Slab**	12m	M		
197.1	**Gnat's Slab Arête**	12m	S		
198	**Marie Celeste**	15m	E1	5b	
199	**Lusitania**	12m	S		
199.1	**Lusitania Direct Finish**	12m	HS	4a	
200	**QE2**	12m	VS	5a	
201	**Titanic**	11m	VS	4b	**
202	**Titanic Direct**	10m	HVS	5a	*

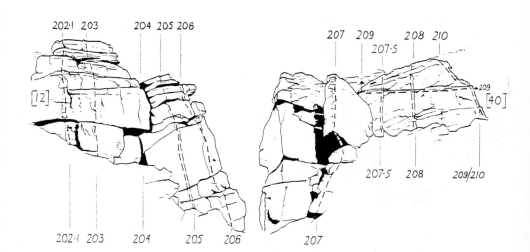

BLOCKHEAD BUTTRESS

202.1	Miss World	9m	HS	4b	
203	Mr Universe	9m	E3	6a	
204	Angus	9m	VD		
205	Sinew Stretch	8m	HVS	5b	
206	Blockhead Direct	8m	HVS	5b	*
207	Headbanger	7m	E1	5c	*
207.5	Prairie Dog	6m	HVS	5b	
208	Scavenger	8m	VS	4c	
209	Sneaking Sally.. (traverse)	10m	VS	4c	
210	Scraps	8m	VS	5a	

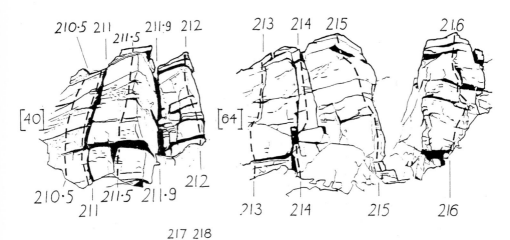

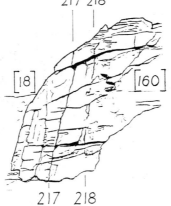

GENESIS BUTTRESS

210.5	Sinister	10m	VS	4c	
211	Left	10m	VD		
211.5	Nice One	10m	VD		
211.9	Corner Crack	8m	VD		
212	Right	8m	HS	4b	
213	49th Parallel	9m	HS	4b	
214	Parallel Cracks	9m	VS	4b	
215	Anniversary Arête	11m	E1	5b	**
216	Grain of Truth	8m	E3	6b	*
217	Genesis	8m	VS	5a	
218	Magazine	7m	VS	4c	

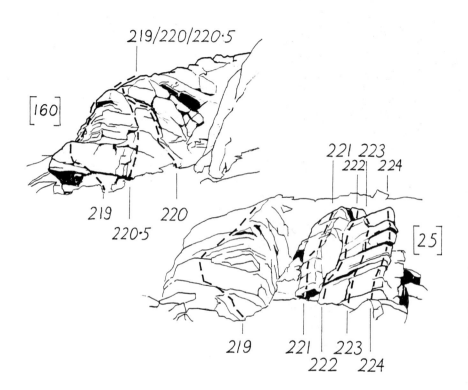

CRACKED WALL BUTTRESS

219	Wall and Slab	11m	VD	
220	Cracked Wall	11m	HVD	
220.5	Cracked Wall Direct	11m	VS	4c
221	Creepy	12m	S	
222	Cringe	8m	VS	4c
223	Crawly	8m	VD	
224	Creepy Crawly	8m	HS	4b

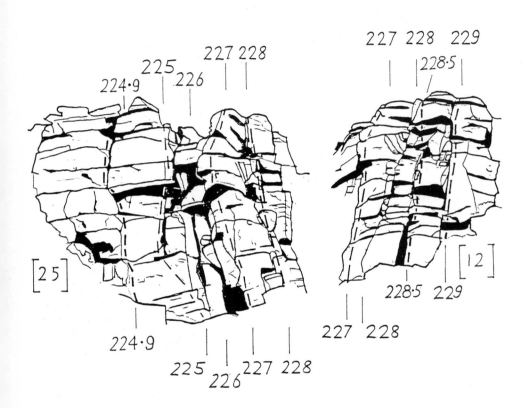

BROKEN BUTTRESS

224.9	Dissuader	15m	HS	4b	
225	Persuader	15m	VS	4c	
226	Burgess Crack	12m	D		
227	Pertinacious	15m	HVS	5b	
228	Broken Buttress	15m	D	-	*
228.5	Broken In	15m	HS		
229	Broken Groove	14m	VD		

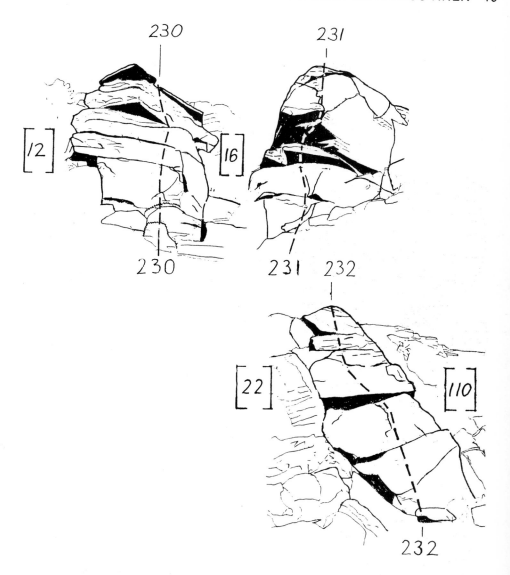

BLOW OUT BUTTRESS   PROWLER BUTTRESS   HEATHER SLAB

230	Blow Out			
231	Prowler	15m	HVS	5b
232	Heather Slab	5m	HVS	5a
		20m	D	

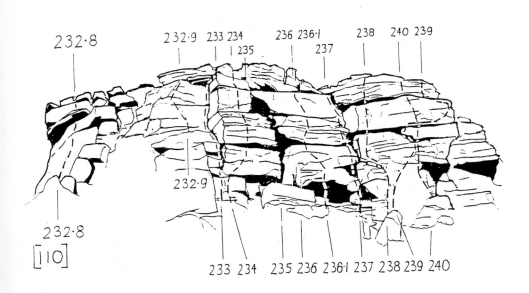

ENCLOSURE BUTTRESS

232.8	Bolt Buttress	6m	VS	4c	
232.9	Warm September	10m	VS	4c	
233	Enclosure Crack	12m	D		
234	Mantelpiece	12m	VS	4c	
235	Central Chimney	16m	M		
236	Central Buttress	18m	VS	4c	*
236.1	Central Buttress Direct	18m	E1	6b	*
237	Centrepiece	15m	VS	4c	
238	The Graduate	13m	E1	5c	
239	Countess Buttress	14m	VS	4b	
240	Haze	13m	HVS	4c	

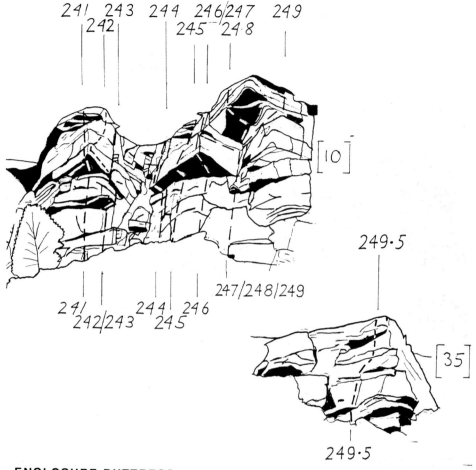

241 243 244 246/247 249
242 245 24·8

10

249·5

247/248/249

241 244 246
242/243 245

249·5

35

ENCLOSURE BUTTRESS

241	Four Winds; Eight Directions	15m	E3	6a
242	Zit	12m	VS	5a
243	Slanting Chimney	11m	VD	
244	Keith's Crack	9m	HS	4b
245	Arsenic Poisoning	8m	HVS	5b
246	Head Over Heels	8m	E3	6a
247	Letter-box	6m	D	
248	Europa	8m	E4	5c
249	Turnover	9m	D	
249.5	Black Attack	7m	E3	6a

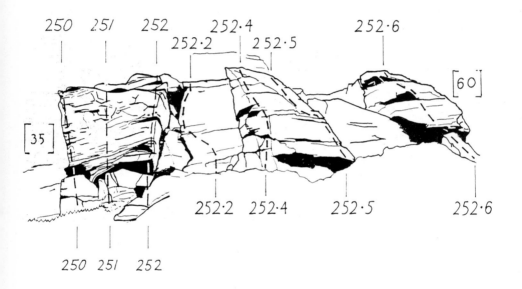

250	Meninblack II	7m	E2	5b
251	Waiting for the Men In Black	6m	HVS	5a
252	Time and Tide	6m	VS	5b
252.2	Naughtical Slab	5m	VS	4c
252.4	High Tide	6m	VS	5a
252.5	No Man	7m	HS	
252.6	The Big C	7m	VS	5a

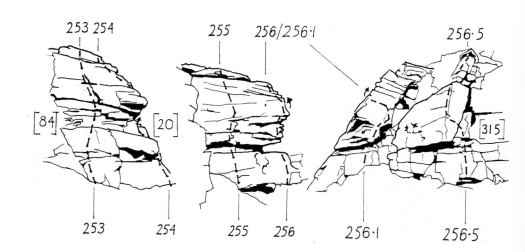

CENTURION'S SLAB

253	Centurion's Slab	10m	M	-	*
254	Duchess	10m	HVS	5b	
255	Trench Deadlock	7m	HVS	4c	
256	Motor Mile (the arête)	7m	HVS	5a	
256.1	Mini Motor Mile	7m	VS	4b	
256.5	Beaky	7m	VS	5a	

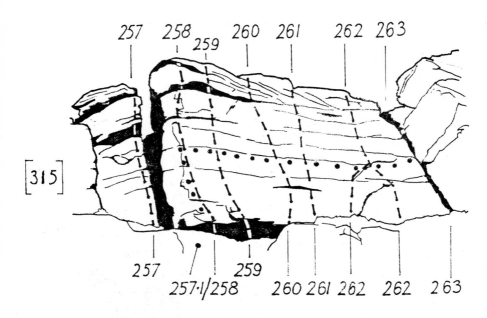

[315]

COUNT'S BUTTRESS

257	**Eden Arête**	6m	S		
257.1	**Insomniac** (traverse)	-	E1	5c	
258	**Nightmare Slab**	9m	E1	5c	*
259	**Dream Boat**	9m	E3	6b	
260	**Daydreamer**	9m	E2	6b	*
261	**Nightrider**	9m	E2	6b	
262	**Sleepwalker**	8m	HVS	6a	
263	**Nightride Corner**	6m	VD		

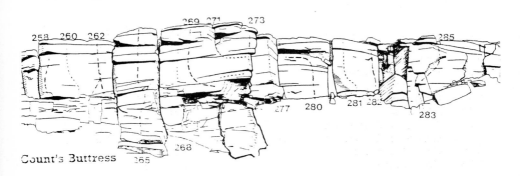

Count's Buttress

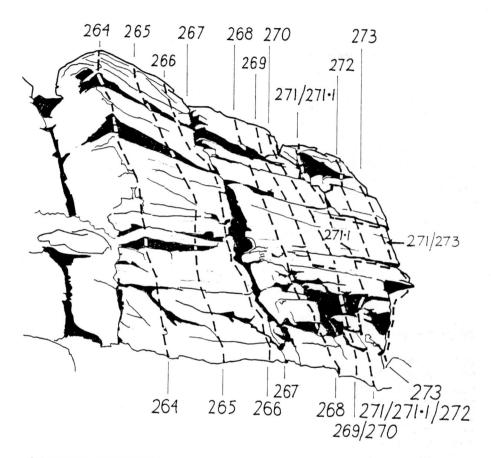

COUNT'S BUTTRESS

264	Out for the Count	13m	E4	6a	
265	The Cool Curl	15m	E6	6b	*
266	Touched	14m	HVS	5c	
267	Count's Chimney	14m	D		*
268	Count's Wall	17m	HVS	5b	
269	Counterblast	16m	E2	5b	
270	Abacus	16m	E2	5b	
271	Count's Buttress	15m	E1	5b	*
271.1	Count's Buttress Direct	14m	E2	5b	
272	Count Me Out	15m	E2	6a	
273	The Count	14m	E1	5c	*

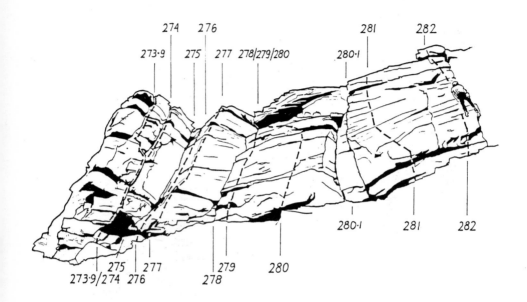

COUNT'S BUTTRESS

273.9	Lost Count	-	HVS	5a	
274	Count's Crack	11m	VS	4c	**
275	B Crack	9m	D		
276	Anxiety Attack 2	9m	E2	5c	
277	Dracula	9m	HVS	5b	
278	Scraped Crack	8m	D	-	
279	Basil Brush	8m	HVS	5a	
280	Lino	9m	VD		
280.1	Prickly Crack	9m	VD		
281	Shirley's Shining Temple	9m	E5	6c	***
282	Shock Horror Slab	9m	E1	6a	*

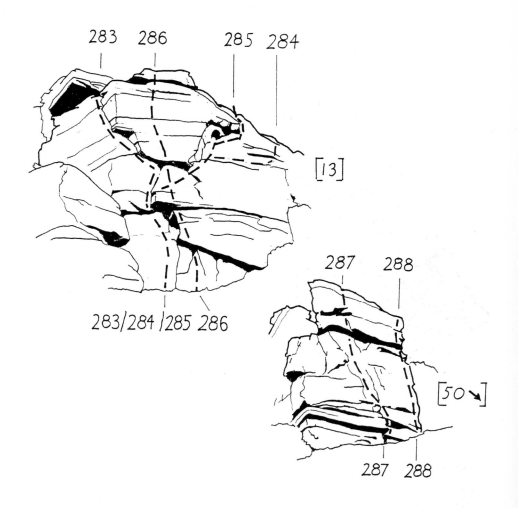

FLAKED BUTTRESS

BON AMI BUTTRESS

283	Flaked Crack	8m	HVD	
284	Flaked Traverse	10m	HVD	
285	The Stretcher	9m	VS	4b
286	The Trickledown Fairy	10m	E5	6b	*
287	Bon Ami	6m	VS	5a
288	Amoeba on the Edge of Time	6m	VS	5b

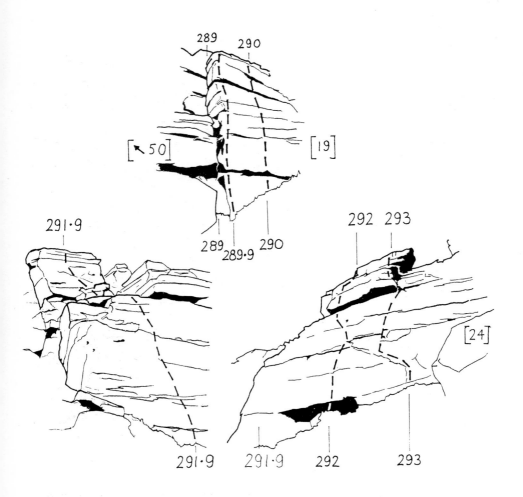

KIT CAT BUTTRESS

289	**Canton**	9m	D	
289.9	**Have a Nice Day**	9m	VS	5a
290	**Kitcat**	9m	VS	5b
291	**Have a Break** (unidentified)	7m	E3	6a
291.9	**Sharpener**	13m	HVS	5a
292	**Protractor**	8m	HVS	5a
293	**Setsquare**	8m	HVD	
294	**Preston's Wall** (unidentified)	11m	HVS	5b

PROTRACTOR BUTTRESS

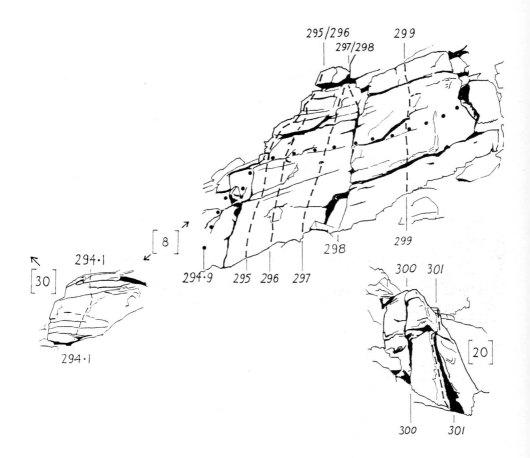

GREYSTOKE BOULDER   D.I.Y. BUTTRESS   TOXIC BUTTRESS

294.1	**The Amazing Harry Greystoke II**	–	VS	5b	
294.9	**Hairless Art** (traverse)	–	HVS	5b	
295	**Black and Decker**	9m	E1	5c	
296	**D.I.Y.**	10m	E3	6a	**
297	**Torture Garden**	10m	E3	6b	**
298	**Grime**	8m	HS	4b	
299	**Sithee**	8m	E1	6a	
300	**Marmite**	5m	HS	4b	
301	**Toxic**	6m	D		

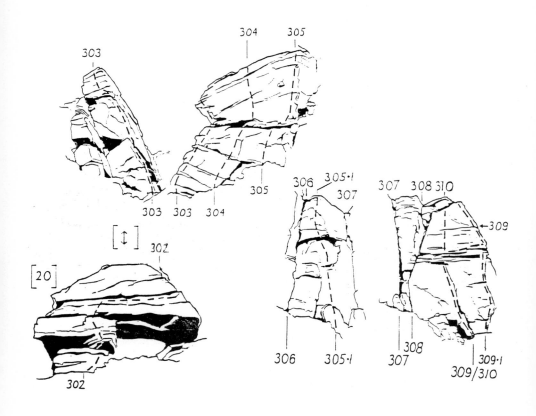

302	Dot's Slab	8m	D	
303	Basil Half-tail	9m	E1	5c
304	Tom-cat Slab	9m	HVS	5b *
305	Skin Grafter	9m	E2	5b
305.1	Non-toxic	9m	VS	4c
306	Short Crack	8m	M	
307	Dry Crack	6m	D	
308	Flute Chimney	8m	D	
309	Ma's Retreat	9m	HVS	5b
309.1	Boobagram	9m	E1	6a
310	Tram Eaters	9m	E2	6a

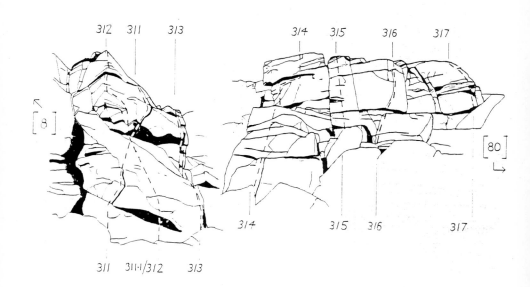

TWO TIER BUTTRESS

311	Surprise	16m	HVS	5b
311.1	Surprise - Direct Start	-	E?	6a
312	Feminist's Breakfast	16m	E4	6a
313	Mother's Day	11m	VS	4c
314	Warlock	12m	HVS	5a
315	Afterthought	11m	HVD	
316	Zero Zero Sputnik	11m	E1	5b
317	Waffti	11m	VD	

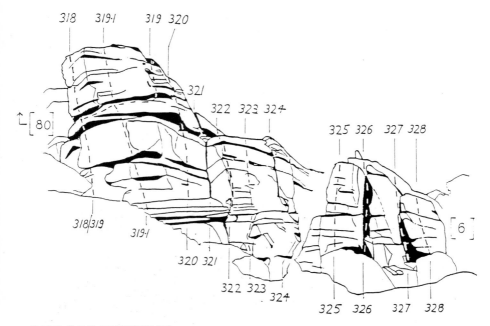

OUTLOOK BUTTRESS

318	The Introvert	8m	E2	5c	
319	Outlook Buttress	8m	HVS	5b	
319.1	Tying the Knot	9m	E3	6a	
320	Look Before You Leap	8m	E1	5c-6c	
321	Outlook Layback	7m	S		
322	A Thousand Natural Shocks	6m	HVS	5c	
323	Weather Report	9m	E5	6c	**
324	Outlook Crack	8m	VS	4c	
325	I Didn't Get Where I am Today	8m	E2	5b	
326	Outlook Chimney	7m	VS	5a	
327	Lookout Flake	7m	S		
328	Splinter	7m	HVS	5c	

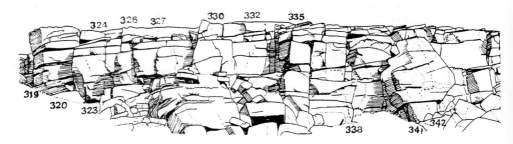

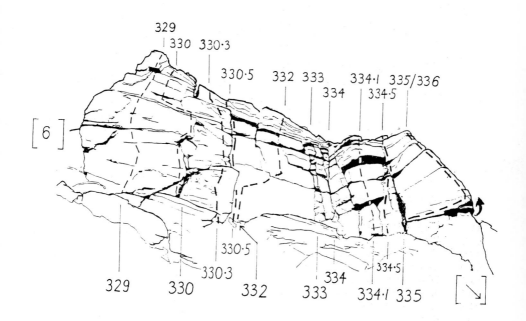

AMPITHEATRE BUTTRESS

329	Tales of Yankee Power	10m	E1	5c	
330	Flaky Wall	10m	HVS	5b	
330.3	Bastille	10	E1	5b	
330.5	Shaky Gully	8m	VD		
332	Amphitheatre Face	8m	VS	5a	
333	Ladder Cracks	8m	D		
334	Ladder Corner	8m	M		
334.1	Tears and Guts	8m	E2	6a	
334.5	Whimper	7m	HVD		
335	Argus	8m	E2	5b	*

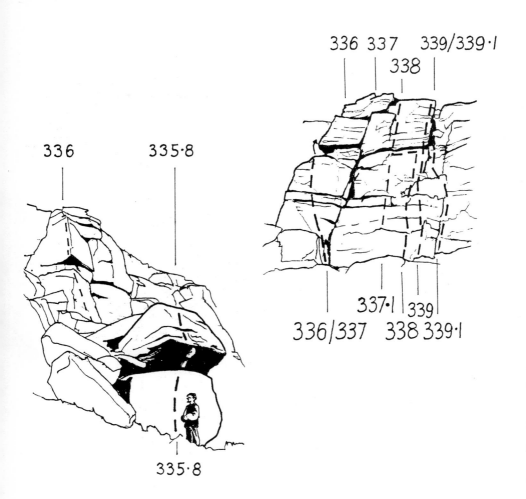

FERN BUTTRESS

335.8 Dijon Dip	6m	E2	6b	
336 Silk	16m	E5	6c	**
337 Fern Crack	16m	VS	4c	**
337.1 Help the Aged (direct start)	-	-	6c	
338 Fern Groove	17m	E2	5c	**
338.1 Help the Aged	-	E2	6c	
339 Smash Your Glasses	9m	E5	6b	**
339.1 Spartacaid	10m	HVS	5a	

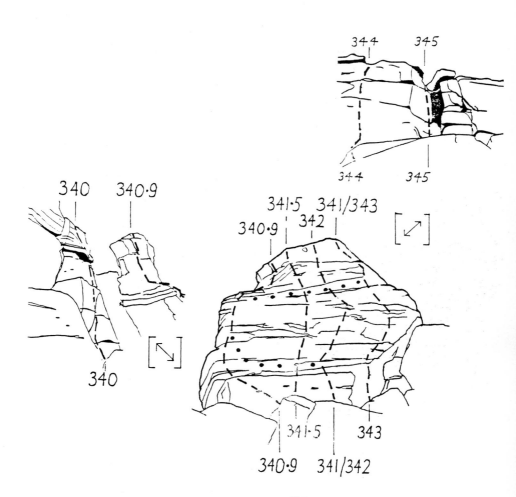

WALL END SLAB

340	Toothcomb	16m	VS	4c	
340.9	Left Over	14m	VS	5a	
341	Wall End Slab (2 traverses)	20m	VS	5a	**
341.5	Wall End Slab Super Duper Direct	14m	E4	5c	*
342	Wall End Slab Direct	14m	E3	5c	*
343	Pure, White and Deadly	12m	E2	5c	
344	Narlavision	7m	HVS	5b	
345	Jammed Stone Chimney	7m	VD		

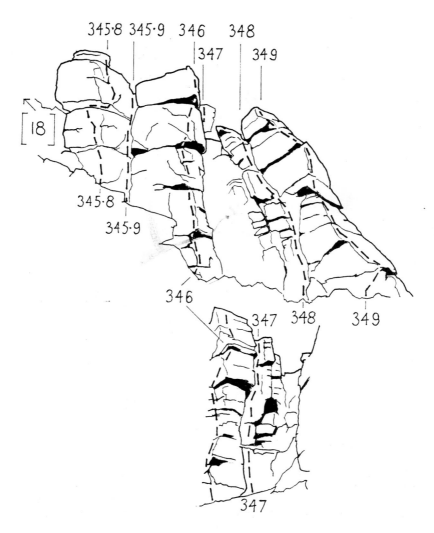

COIGN BUTTRESS

345.8	**Mate**	7m	E1	5b
345.9	**Cheque**	7m	VD	
346	**Giro**	9m	E2	5c
347	**P.O. Crack**	8m	HS	4b
348	**Slanting Chimney**	10m	S	
349	**The Coign**	20m	S	

350 351 352 353

OUTLOOK SLAB

350	Outlook Slab	18m	VS	4c
351	Wall End Crack	18m	S 22/09/94 O	
352	Death and Night and Blood	18m	E1	5b
353	Wall End Flake Crack	20m	VS	4c

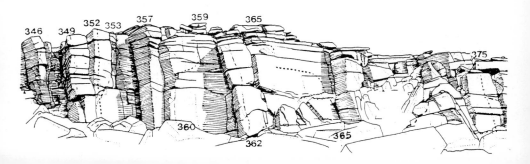

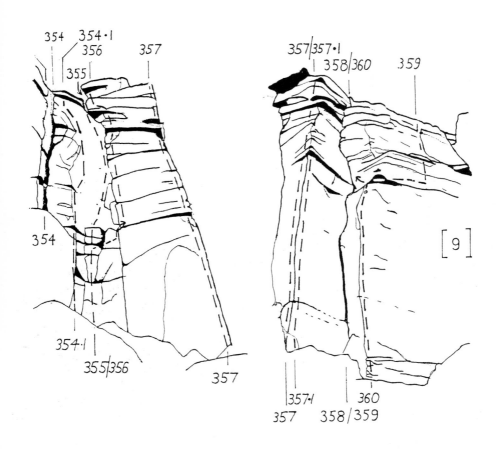

GOLIATH'S GROOVE

354	Wall End Holly Tree Crack	20m	HS	4b	
354.1	I Never Said It Was Any Good	20m	E1	5b	
355	Helfenstein's Struggle	20m	D	-	*
356	Dark Angel	21m	HVS	5b	
357	Archangel	21m	E3	5b	***
357.1	Don	-	E4	5c	
358	Goliath's Groove	21m	HVS	5a	***
359	Doncaster's Route	21m	HVS	5a	
360	Ulysses	20m	E6	6b	***

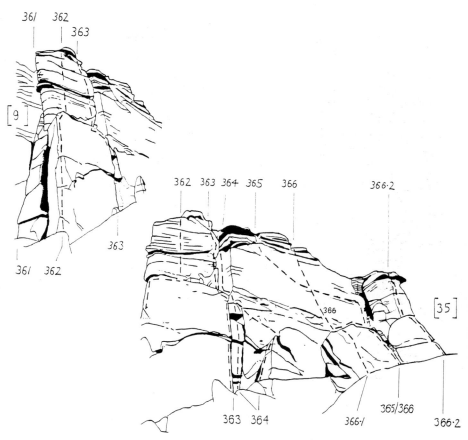

FAIRY STEPS

361	Hollybush Gully Left	20m	S		
362	White Wand	23m	E5	6a	***
363	Leaps and Bounds	20m	E1	5b	
364	Hollybush Gully Right	20m	M		
365	Fairy Steps	15m	VS	4a	**
366	Gnome Man's Land	20m	E4	6b	
366.1	Gnome Direct Start	-	-	6b	
366.2	Double Act	12m	HVS	5c	
366.3	Wall End Girdle	-	VS	4c	
	(traverse not shown 'obvious line' to 351)				

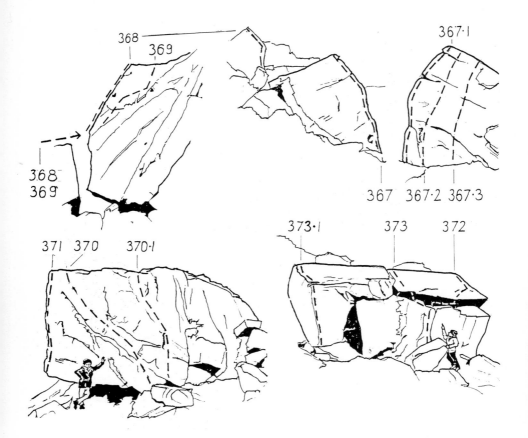

THE BOULDERS - for simple approach refer to Hollin Bank Access Point 3.

367	**Crescent Arête**	7m	HVS	5b	**
367.1	**Sideslip**	-	E2	6a	
367.2	**Sidelined**	-	E2	6b	
367.3	**Brushed**	-	E2	6c	
368	**Breadline**	4m	E4	6b	*
369	**Big Air**	4m	E6	6b	
370	**Not To Be Taken Away**	8m	E2	6a	***
370.1	**Rotor**	-	-	5c	
371	**Careless Torque**	6m	E6	7a	**
372	**The Photograph**	7m	E3	5c	
373	**Video Nasty**	6m	E1	6a	
373.1	**Adult Only**	-	E1	6b	

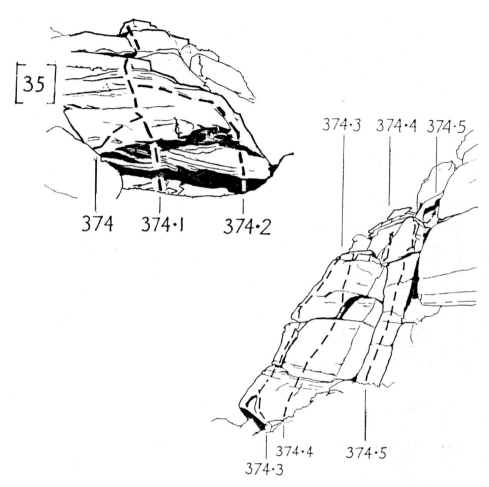

SPUR SLAB

374	**Spur Slab**	11m D	
374.1	**Left Spur**	11m -	6b
374.2	**Right Spur**	11m -	6b
374.3	**Hot Spur**	11m VS	4c
374.4	**Stirrup**	11m HS	4b
374.5	**Ride Him Cowboy**	14m VS	5a

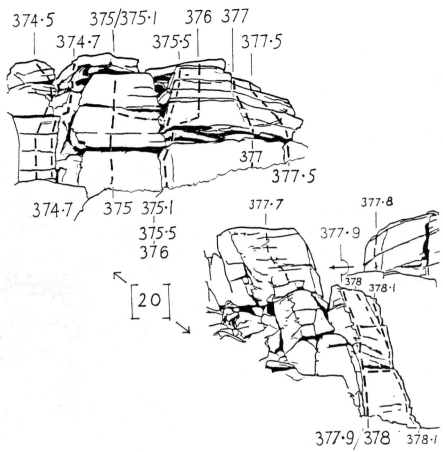

SATIN BUTTRESS

FINA BUTTRESS

374.7	Corduroy	8m	VS	4c	
375	Satin	8m	E3	6b	*
375.1	Living at the Speed	9m	E1	5b	
375.5	Mark Devalued	7m	VS	4b	
376	Mark's Slab	8m	VS	5a	
377	Pullover	10m	HVS	5b	*
377.5	Roll Neck	6m	VS	5a	
377.7	A Day Without Pay	5m	E6	6c	*
377.8	Louis the Loon	5m	E2	6a	
377.9	Unleaded	9m	S		
378	Fina	15m	HVS	5b	*
378.1	Four Star	15m	E3	6b	

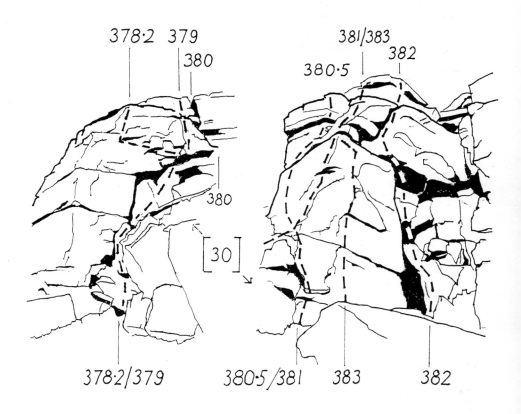

378·2 379
380

381/383
382

380·5

380

[30]

378·2/379

380·5/381   383

382

ESSO BUTTRESS

378.2	Hot and Bothered	9m	E3	6b	*
379	Centaur	8m	E1	5c	*
380	Additive Chimney	10m	VD		
380.5	Stealth	12m	VS	4c	
381	Cinturato	14m	E1	5b	*
382	Esso Extra	17m	E1	5b	
383	Grace and Danger	15m	E6	6c	**

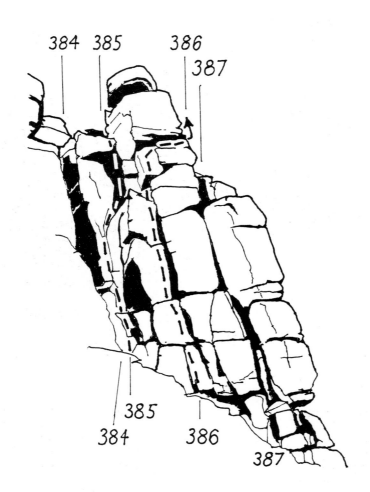

TOWER BUTTRESS

384	Waterloo Branch	14m	HS	
385	Tower Gully	14m	S	
386	Tower Crack	24m	HVS	5a	*
387	Tower Chimney	20m	HVS	5b	*

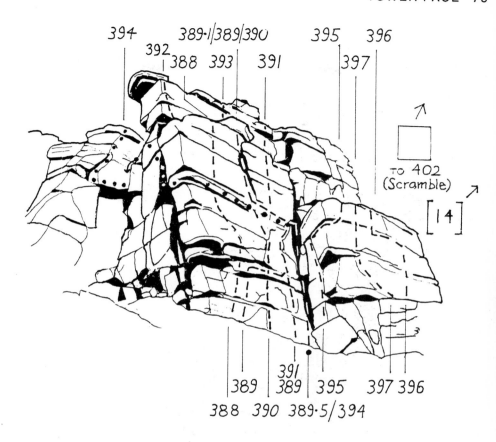

TOWER FACE

388	Indian Summer	25m	E5	6b	**
389	Tower Face	25m	HVS	5a	**
389.5	Tower Face Indirect	25m	VS	4c	*
390	Tower Face Direct	25m	E2	5b	
391	Scrole Not Dole	25m	E5	6a	
392	Miserable Miracle				
	(from high ledge)	7m	HVS	5b	
393	Nihilistic Narl				
	(from high ledge)	6m	E4	6b	
394	Tower Traverse	50m	E1	5b	
395	Stretcher Case	11m	E2	5c	*
396	Nuke the Midges	9m	E1	5c	
397	Scuppered	7m	E4	6a	

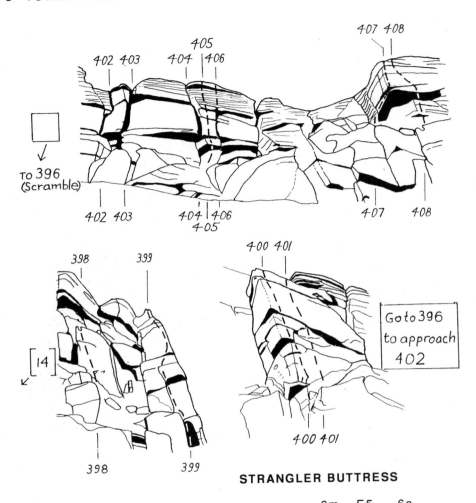

STRANGLER BUTTRESS

398	Swooper	6m	E5	6a
399	Neutrons For Old	13m	E2	5c
400	The Strangler	12m	E4	5c	*
401	Skidoo	12m	E6	6c	*
402	Terrace Gully	8m	VD	
403	The Chute	10m	S	
404	The Mangler	10m	E1	5c
405	Foetus on the Eiger	10m	E1	6a
406	Crescent	10m	VS	5a
407	Grooved Arête	8m	S	
408	Anji	10m	VS	4c

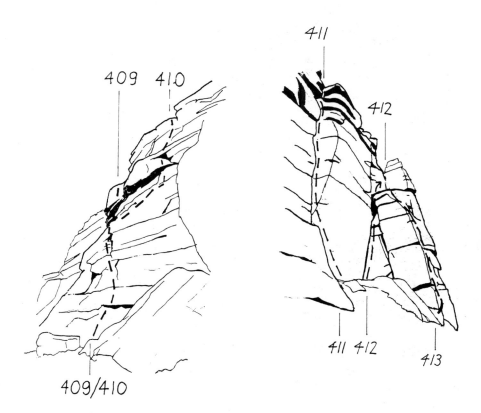

409 410

409/410

411

412

411 412 413

OBSTINANCE BUTTRESS

409	Obstinance	14m	VS	4c
410	Slab and Crack	14m	VS	5a
411	Gardener's Groove	10m	HS	4b
412	Compost Corner	8m	D	

413/414   415/415·2   415·4/415·6

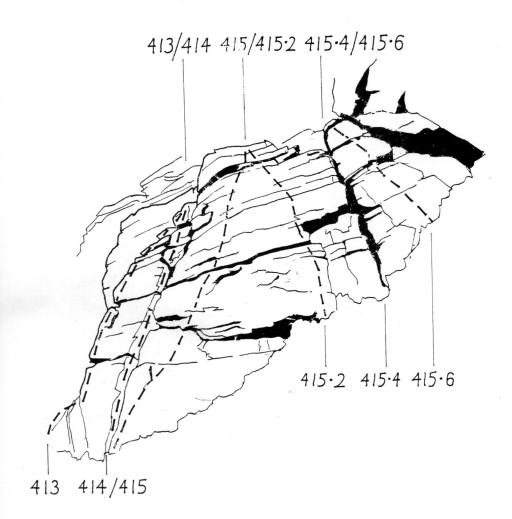

415·2   415·4   415·6

413   414/415

GARDENER'S BUTTRESS

413	Percy's Prow	8m	S	
414	Gardener's Crack	10m	D	
415	Pizza Slab	10m	S	
415.2	Cheapest Topping	9m	VS	4c
415.4	Poor Pizza	10m	D	
415.6	Nasty Green Dwarf	8m	VS	4c

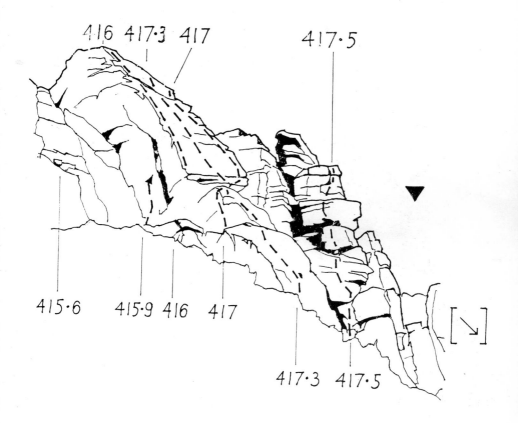

SCORPION SLAB

415.9 Paping About... (L slit in chimney)	8m	VS	4c	
416 Small Dreams	11m	E3	6a	
417 Scorpion Slab	11m	VD		
417.3 Big Screams	14m	E1	5c	*
417.5 Stacked Blocks	12m	VS	4b	

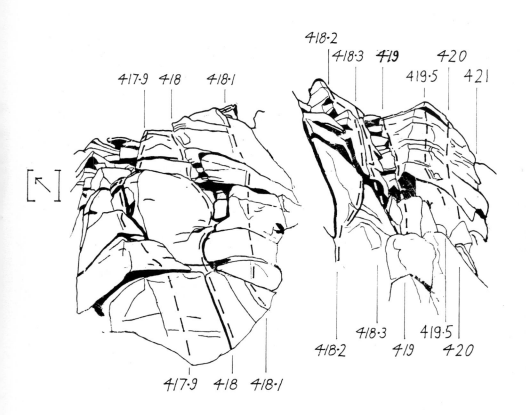

HERCULES BUTTRESS

417.9	Gripe Fruit Juice	14m	HVS 5a	
418	Hercules Crack	14m	VD	
418.1	Shelf Life	14m	E3 5c	*
418.2	Squally Showers	10m	VS 4c	
418.3	Edale Trip (Beyond Hope)	10m	E3 6a	
419	Mercury Crack	11m	VD	
419.5	My Herald of Free Enterprise	10m	E6 6c	
420	The Hathersage Trip	10m	E4 6a	**

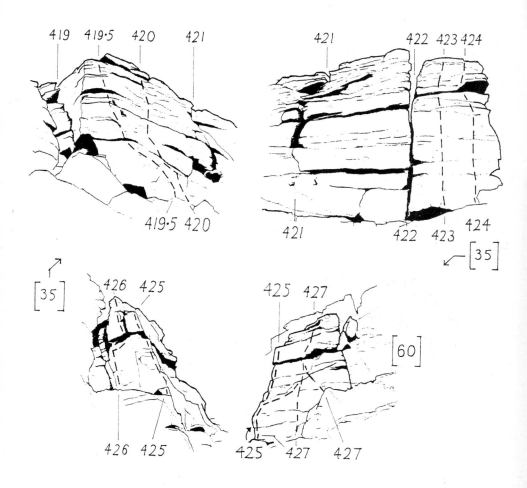

SEESAW BUTTRESS

419.5	My Herald of Free Enterprise	10m	E6	6c	
420	The Hathersage Trip	10m	E4	6a	**
421	Overhanging Crack	10m	VS	5a	
422	Corner Crack	8m	HS	4c	
423	National Breakdown	8m	E3	6c	
424	Big Bob's Bazzer	8m	HVS	5a	
425	Seesaw	14m	VS	4c	*
426	Fulcrum	10m	HVS	5a	
427	Margery Daw	10m	HVS	5b	

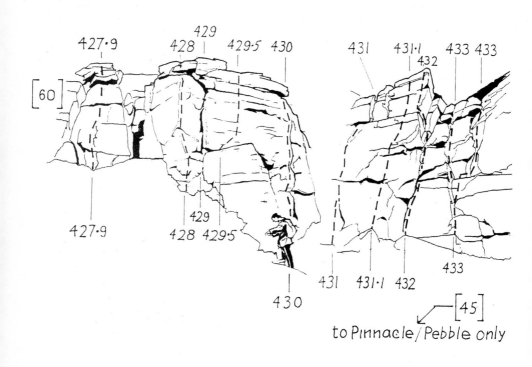

to Pinnacle/Pebble only

TAURUS BUTTRESS

427.9	**Horn**	9m	VS	5a
428	**Too Cold to be Bold**	13m	E2	6b
429	**Taurus Crack**	11m	HS	4c
429.5	**Star Trek**	10m	E5	6c
430	**Valhalla**	10m	VS	5a	*
431	**Pegasus Wall**	10m	VS	4c	*
431.1	**Back to School**	12m	HVS	5b
432	**Pegasus Rib**	13m	HVS	5a	*
433	**Flake Gully**	10m	M	

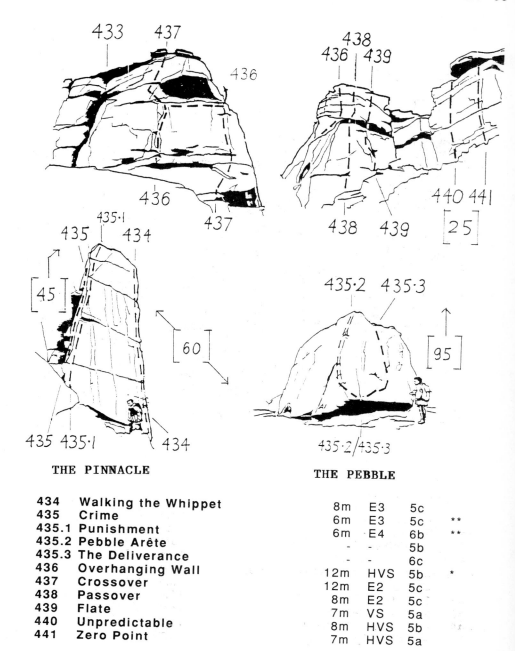

THE PINNACLE

THE PEBBLE

434	Walking the Whippet	8m	E3	5c
435	Crime	6m	E3	5c	**
435.1	Punishment	6m	E4	6b	**
435.2	Pebble Arête	-	-	5b
435.3	The Deliverance	-	-	6c
436	Overhanging Wall	12m	HVS	5b	*
437	Crossover	12m	E2	5c
438	Passover	8m	E2	5c
439	Flate	7m	VS	5a
440	Unpredictable	8m	HVS	5b
441	Zero Point	7m	HVS	5a

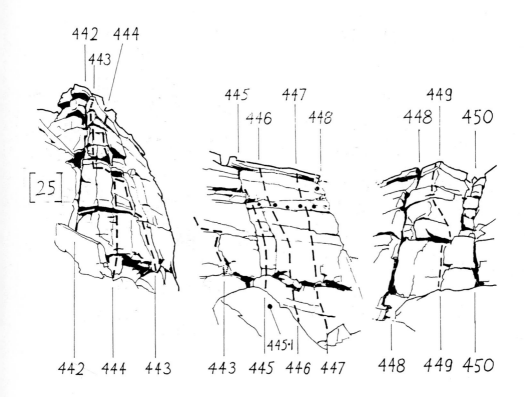

PARADISE WALL

442	**Paradise Lost**		13m	D	
443	**Paradise Arête**		13m	VS	4c
444	**Parasite**		13m	HVS	5a
445	**Paradise Wall**		13m	VS	4c	**
445.1	**Milton's Meander** (traverse)		16m	VS	4c
446	**Comet**		13m	E3	5c
447	**Comus**		13m	E4	6a	*
448	**Paradise Crack**		14m	D	
449	**American Gritfeati**		14m	HVS	5b
450	**Sand Gully**		14m	D	

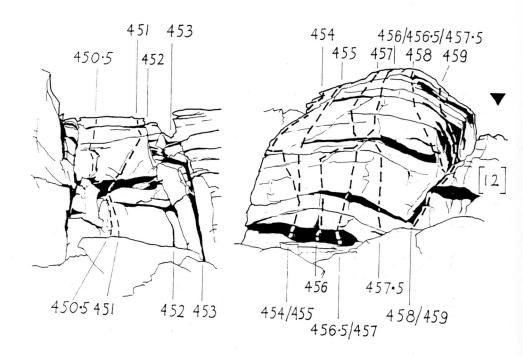

BILLIARD BUTTRESS

450.5	Quartz	14m	HVS	4c	
451	Silica	14m	E2	5c	**
452	Sand Crack	11m	S		
453	Curved Crack	11m	VD		*
454	Billiard Buttress	22m	HVS	5a	**
455	Pot Black	22m	E2	5b	**
456	Millsom's Minion	22m	E1	5b	**
456.5	Millsom's Direct	22m	E3	5c	
457	In-off	22m	E3	5c	**
457.5	Back in the Y.M.C.A.	17m	E4	6c	**
458	A Problem of Coagulation	22m	E3	5c	
459	Cue	23m	HVS	5b	**

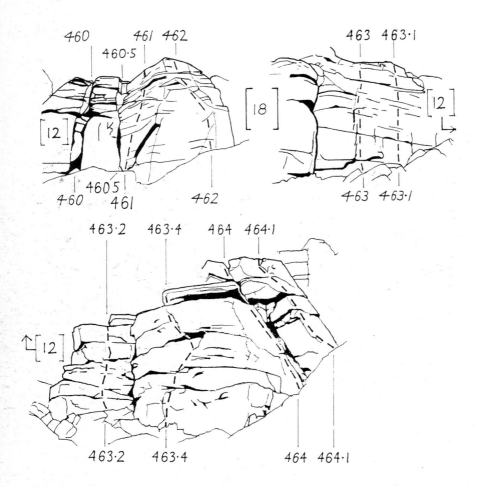

CANNON BUTTRESS

460	Left Pool Crack	8m	D	
460.5	Right Pool Crack	8m	D	
461	Between the Two	8m	HVS	5b
462	Pool Wall	8m	VS	4c
463	Tridymite Slab	7m	VS	5a
463.1	Mitch Pitch	7m	HVS	5b
463.2	Modesty	5m	VS	4c
463.4	Elephant in the Doghouse	8m	E1	5b
464	Cannon	8m	D	
464.1	Turnbull's Trajectory	6m	S	4a

Right: 341: Wall End Slab

TYPICAL STANAGE GRIT

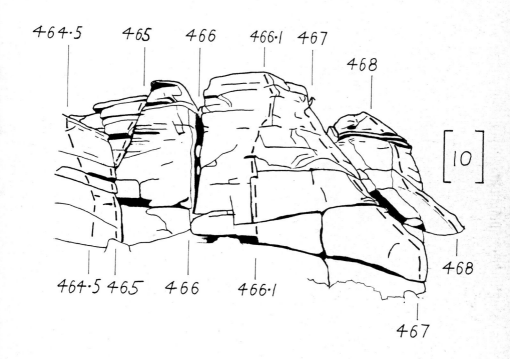

464.5   465   466   466.1   467   468

[10]

464.5   465   466   466.1   468

467

SYMBIOSIS BUTTRESS

464.5	Turnbull Missed	6m	VS	4b
465	Slanting Crack	8m	HS	4b
466	Straight Ahead	8m	D	
466.1	Blue Fluff	9m	E4	5c
467	Symbiosis	10m	VS	4c
468	Nephron	8m	VS	4c

Left: 497: Left Unconquerable

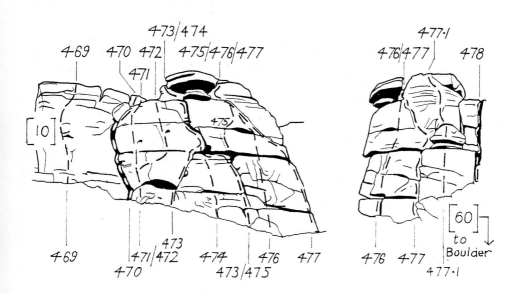

WALL BUTTRESS

469	**Boys Will Be Boys**	8m	E6	6c	**
470	**Capstone Chimney**	10m	D		
471	**Badly Bitten**	10m	E4	6a	
472	**Moribund**	10m	E3	5c	*
473	**Wall Buttress**	12m	VS	5a	*
474	**Walrus Butter**	6m	E4	6b	
475	**Direct Loss**	6m	E4	6a	**
476	**Improbability Drive**	12m	E3	6a	*
477	**Namenlos**	13m	E1	5a	**
477.1	**Memory Loss**	13m	HVS	5b	

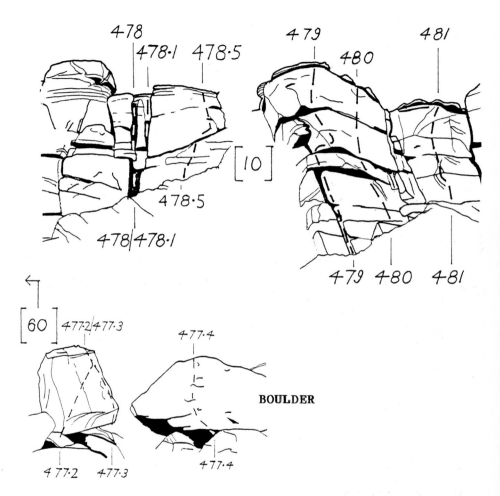

BOULDER

AUGUST BUTTRESS

477.2	**Editor's Vaseline**	4m	HVS	5b
477.3	**Direct Start**	-	E1	6a
477.4	**Fear and Loathing**	4m	E3	5c
478	**Holly Crack**	7m	VD	
478.1	**Straw Crack**	7m	S	
478.5	**Short Straw**	7m	VS	4c
479	**August Arête**	14m	HVS	5a
480	**Telli**	10m	E3	6a	*
481	**Bumblies in Red Socks**	7m	E3	5c

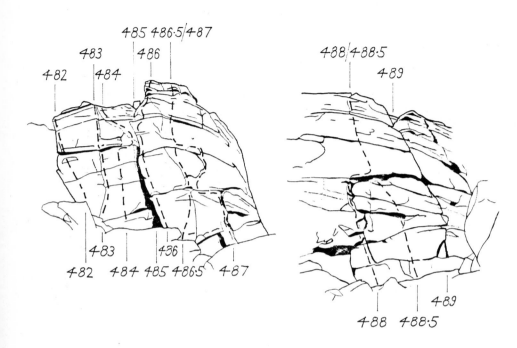

CALVARY BUTTRESS

482	**Vision Set**	11m	E1	5b	
483	**Michelle My Belle**	11m	E3	6a	
484	**Traversty**	11m	HVS	5c	
485	**Rib Chimney**	13m	D		
486	**Nightsalt**	15m	E4	6c	*
486.5	**Calvary Direct**	15m	E5	6a	
487	**Calvary**	19m	E4	6a	**
488	**Defying Destiny**	19m	E5	6b	**
488.5	**Defying Destiny Direct**	-	-	6b	

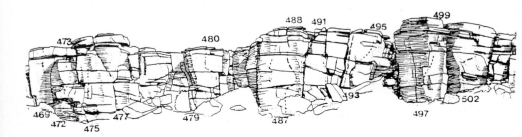

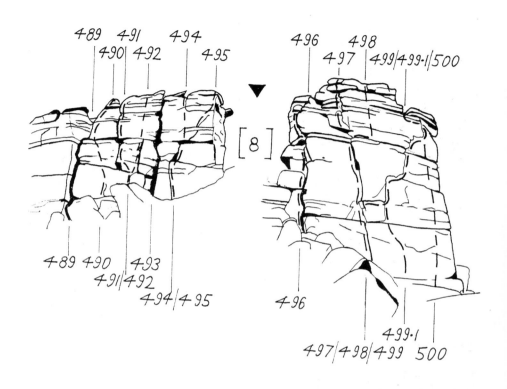

THE UNCONQUERABLES

489	Chockstone Chimney	13m	M		
490	Plugging the Gap	13m	HVS	5a	
491	Cleft Wall Route 1	13m	VD		
492	Early Starter	13m	E1	5b	
493	Cleft Wall Route 2	13m	S		
494	Lucky Strike	13m	E1	5b	
495	Ritornel	13m	HVS	5a	
496	The Little Unconquerable	12m	HVS	5a	*
497	The Left Unconquerable	17m	E1	5b	***
498	Vanquished	17m	E5	6b	
499	The Right Unconquerable	17m	HVS	5a	***
499.1	Direct Start	-	-	6a	
500	Monday Blue	17m	E2	5b	

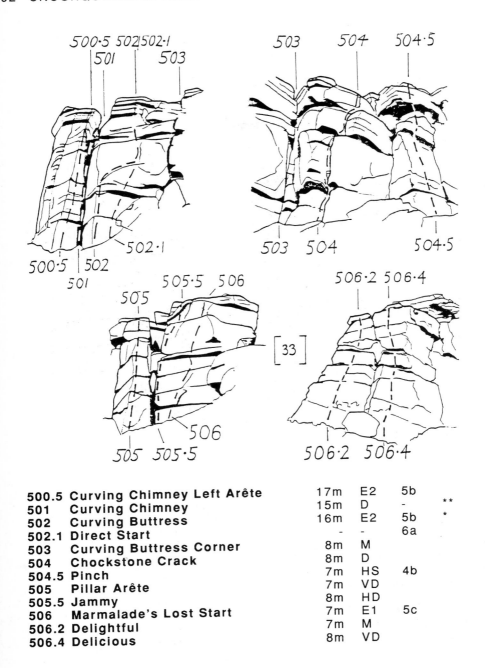

500.5	Curving Chimney Left Arête	17m	E2	5b	**
501	Curving Chimney	15m	D	-	
502	Curving Buttress	16m	E2	5b	*
502.1	Direct Start	-	-	6a	
503	Curving Buttress Corner	8m	M		
504	Chockstone Crack	8m	D		
504.5	Pinch	7m	HS	4b	
505	Pillar Arête	7m	VD		
505.5	Jammy	8m	HD		
506	Marmalade's Lost Start	7m	E1	5c	
506.2	Delightful	7m	M		
506.4	Delicious	8m	VD		

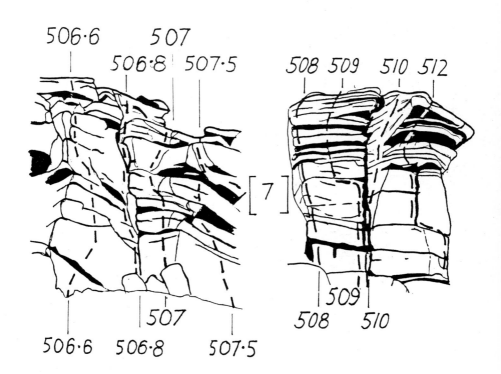

TWIN TOWERS BUTTRESS

506.6	Delovely	7m	HS	4b
506.8	Delirious	7m	D	
507	Scoop and Corner	7m	M	
507.5	Tumble Down	8m	VS	4c
508	Tower Block	10m	E3	6b
509	The Watch-tower	13m	HVS	5b
510	Right Wall	13m	S	

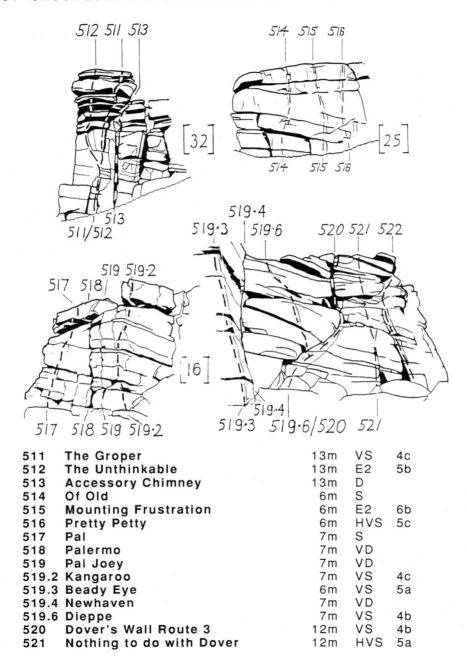

511	The Groper	13m	VS	4c
512	The Unthinkable	13m	E2	5b
513	Accessory Chimney	13m	D	
514	Of Old	6m	S	
515	Mounting Frustration	6m	E2	6b
516	Pretty Petty	6m	HVS	5c
517	Pal	7m	S	
518	Palermo	7m	VD	
519	Pal Joey	7m	VD	
519.2	Kangaroo	7m	VS	4c
519.3	Beady Eye	6m	VS	5a
519.4	Newhaven	7m	VD	
519.6	Dieppe	7m	VS	4b
520	Dover's Wall Route 3	12m	VS	4b
521	Nothing to do with Dover	12m	HVS	5a

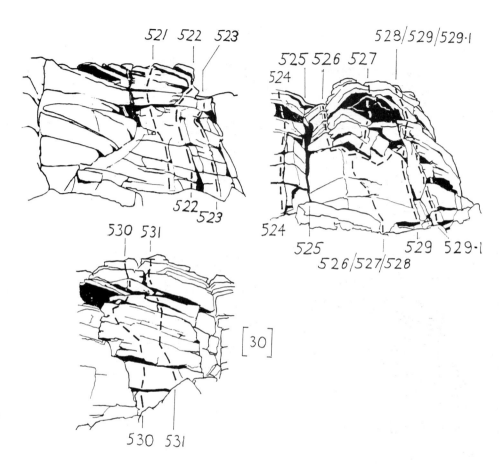

DOVER'S WALL

CLEFT WING BUTTRESS

522	Dover's Wall, Route 2	12m	HVS	5a
523	Dover's Wall, Route 1	12m	HVD	
524	Dover's Wall, Route 4	11m	VS	4b
525	Wing Buttress Gully	12m	D	
526	Wing Buttress	13m	VS	4b
527	5.9 Finish	12m	E1	5b
528	Cleft Wing	12m	VS	5b
529	Cleft Wing Superdirect	12m	VS	4c
529.1	Trimming the Beard	11m	E2	6a
530	Spearing the Bearded Clam	11m	E2	6a
531	Wing Wall	11m	M	

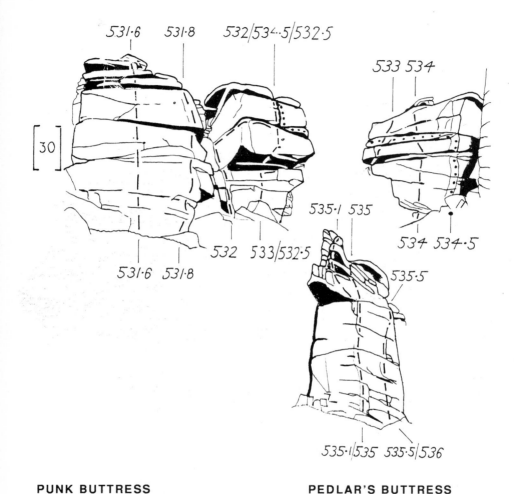

PUNK BUTTRESS

PEDLAR'S BUTTRESS

531.6 Jon's Route	9m	VS	4b	
531.8 Eyes	9m	VS	4c	
532 The Punk	10m	VS	4b	*
532.5 Shine On	9m	E7	6c	
533 BAW's Crawl	10m	HVS	5a	***
534 Punklet	9m	HVS	5c	*
534.5 Public Image (traverse)	10m	VS	4c	
535 Pedlar's Rib	11m	E1	5c	*
535.1 Non-stop Pedalling	-	E2	6a	
535.5 Grope Slope	-	E1	5c	

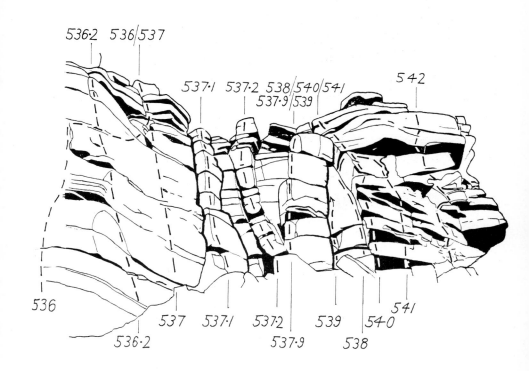

PEDLAR'S SLAB

536	Pedlar's Arête		
536.2	Keep Pedalling		
537	Pedlar's Slab		
537.1	Top Block Rock		
537.2	Recess Rib		
537.3	Pisa Pillar		
538	Pisa Crack		
539	Hidden Crack		
540	Plastic Dream		
541	Tarzan Boy		

VERANDAH BUTTRESS

11m	HVS	5b	
10m	E2	5c	
11m	HVS	5c	*
10m	VD		
10m	D		
10m	HS	4b	
11m	HVD	-	*
10m	VD		
10m	E3	6a	
10m	E3	6a	

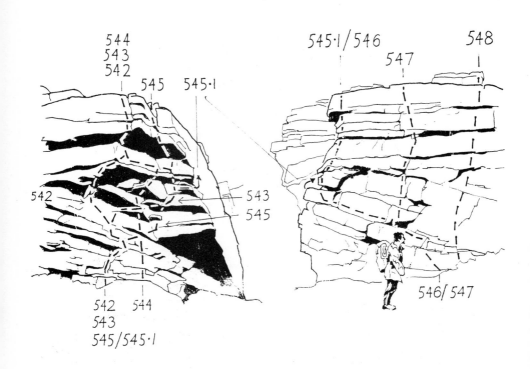

VERANDAH BUTTRESS

542	Off With His Head	13m	E4	6a	**
543	The Guillotine	13m	E3	5c	**
544	Guillotine Direct	13m	E4	6b	***
545	The Old Dragon	12m	E1	5b	
545.1	Mary Whitehouse	-	-	6b	
546	Verandah Buttress	12m	HVD	5b	*
547	Butcher Crack	11m	HVS	5b	

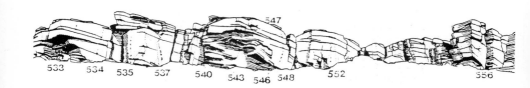

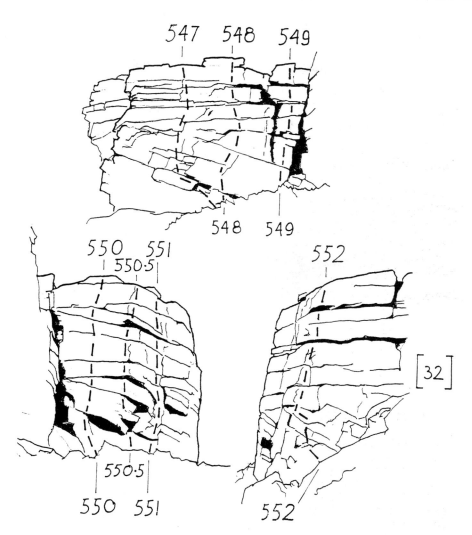

VERANDAH BUTTRESS

548	Greengrocer Wall	11m	HVS	5c	*
549	Verandah Cracks	8m	D		
550	Verandah Wall	10m	VS	4c	
550.5	Cocktail	9m	VS	4c	
551	Verandah Pillar	10m	HS	4b	*
552	The Confectioner	8m	VS	5a	

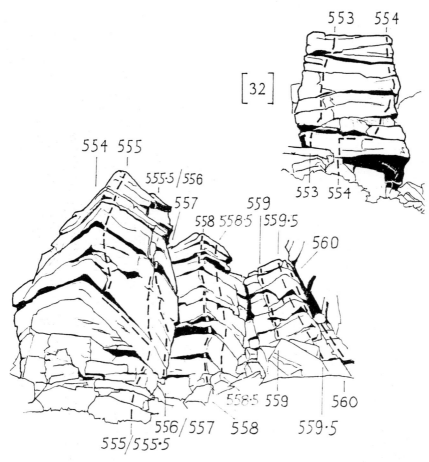

INTERMEDIATE BUTTRESS

553	Intermediate Buttress	10m	VD		
554	The Nose	10m	VS	4b	*
555	Second Wind	11m	HVS	5c	
555.5	Swings (direct start)	-	-	5c	
556	The Roundabout	12m	HVS	5b	
557	Turf Crack	10m	VD		
558	Little Tower	8m	HS		
558.5	49 Bikinis	9m	HVS	5a	
559	Beads	7m	S		
559.5	Trinket	7m	S		
560	Narrowing Chimney	7m	S		

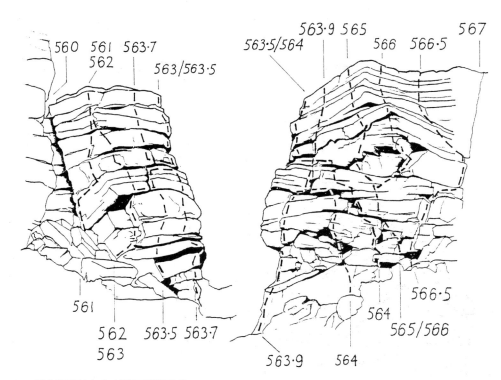

MARTELLO BUTTRESS

561	Vanishing Point	10m	VS	4c	
562	Zel	13m	VS	4b	
563	Byne's Route	15m	S		
563.5	Choux	15m	E2	6a	
563.7	Choux Fleur	15m	E1	5c	
564	Martello Buttress	17m	HS		
565	The Scoop (Ozymandias)	15m	HVS	5a	***
566	Bloodshot	15m	E3	5c	
566.5	Original Scoop	15m	VS	4c	

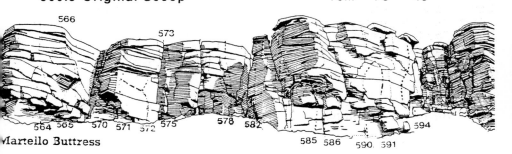

Martello Buttress

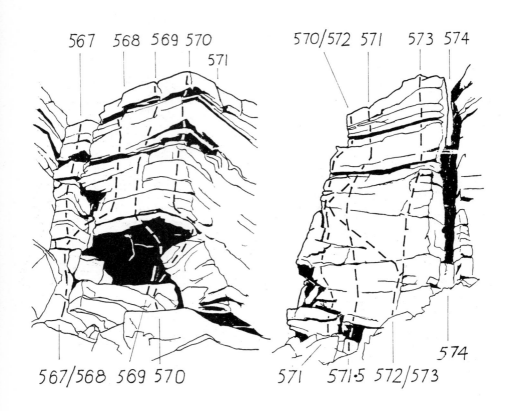

567   568 569 570

571

570/572 571   573 574

567/568 569 570

571   571·5 572/573

574

SALIVA BUTTRESS

567	Martello Cracks	12m	M		
568	Mistella	12m	VD		
569	Wax Museum	12m	HVS	5b	
570	Phlegethoa	12m	HVS	5c	*
571	Fading Star (After the Fire)	13m	E2	6a	*
571.5	Fading Star direct start	-	-	6b	
572	Saliva	13m	HVS	5a	*
573	Ashes	12m	E3	5c	*
574	Devil's Chimney	13m	D	-	**

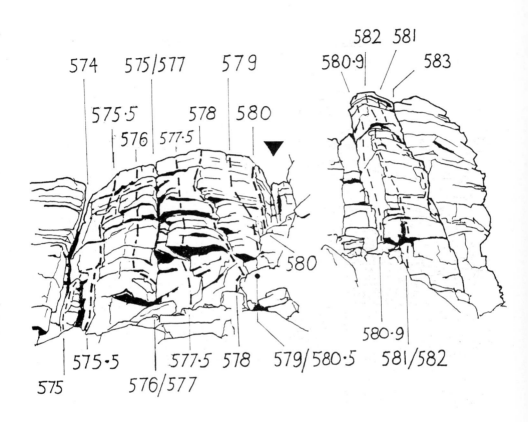

LOUISIANA RIB

575	Step-ladder Crack (The Styx)	15m	VS	4c	**
575.5	Step-ladder Crack (direct)	14m	HVS	5c	
576	Dark Water	14m	E3	6b	
577	Hell Crack	13m	VS	4b	**
577.5	Still in Limbo	13m	E1	5b	
578	Heaven Crack	10m	VD		
579	Lethe	10m	HVS	5a	
580	Jean's Line	10m	VS	4b	
580.5	The Aeneid (traverse to 562)	30m	VS	5a	
580.9	Gathering Gloom	10m	E1	5c	
581	The Louisiana Rib	18m	VS	4c	*
582	Acheron	17m	E1	5b	*

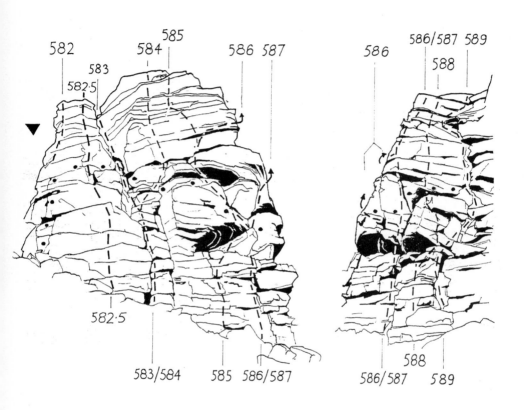

MISSISSIPPI BUTTRESS

582.5	The Levee	17m	HVS	5b	
583	Mississippi Chimney	18m	VD	-	**
584	African Herbs	18m	E2	5c	
585	Dark Continent	18m	E1	5c	**
586	Congo Corner	23m	HVS	5b	***
586.9	Nairobi	-	E4	6a	
587	The Link (Congo Corner Direct)	21m	HVS	5b	***
588	The Mersey Variant	21m	E2	5c	
589	Missisippi Buttress Direct	21m	VS	4c	***

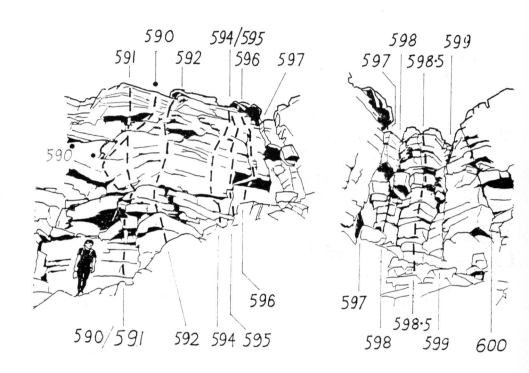

MISSISSIPPI BUTTRESS

590	Mississippi Variant		21m	E1	5b	*
591	Stanleyville		21m	E4	5c	**
592	Puzzlelock		21m	E4	6a	*
593	Ferryboat Highway (traverse)		30m	HVS	5b	
594	Morrison's Redoubt		17m	E1	5b	*
595	Melancholy Witness		17m	E3	6a	
596	Amazon Crack		13m	S	-	*
597	Fallen Pillar Chimney		11m	VD		
598	Fairy Castle Crack		11m	D		
598.5	Pixie		12m	VS	5a	
599	Fairy Chimney		11m	D		

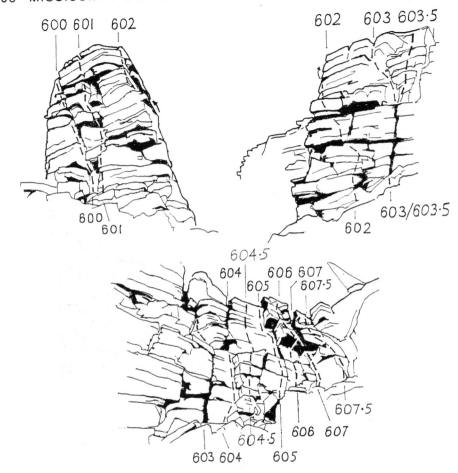

BALCONY BUTTRESS

600	Balcony Climb	12m	HVD		
601	Balcony Cracks	12m	S		
602	Balcony Buttress	17m	S	-	***
603	The Flue	14m	VD		
603.5	Big Yin	14m	VS	4c	
604	Scoop Crack	14m	VD		
604.5	Rib and Face	12m	HVS	4c	
605	Balcony Corner	9m	D		
606	Upanover	8m	VS	5b	
607	Upanover Crack	8m	S		
607.5	Twinkle Toes	8m	M		

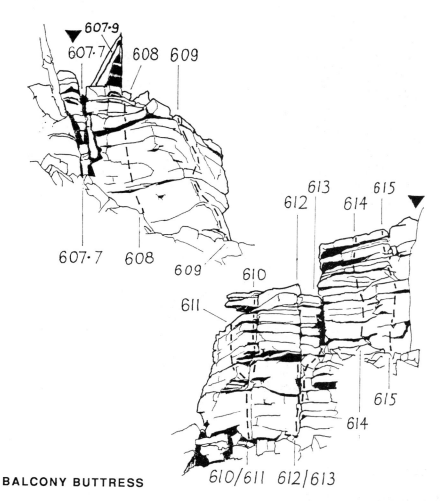

BALCONY BUTTRESS

607.7	Green Needle Gully descent	–	–		
607.9	Savage Amusement	long	E2	5c	
608	M Route	11m	VS	4c	
609	N Route	11m	HS	4a	
610	Agony Crack	11m	HVS	5a	**
611	Regret	11m	E2	5c	
612	Thrombosis	11m	VS	4c	
613	Rigor Mortis	11m	HS	4b	
614	Paralysis	11m	VS	4c	
615	Boris the Bold	11m	VS	4c	

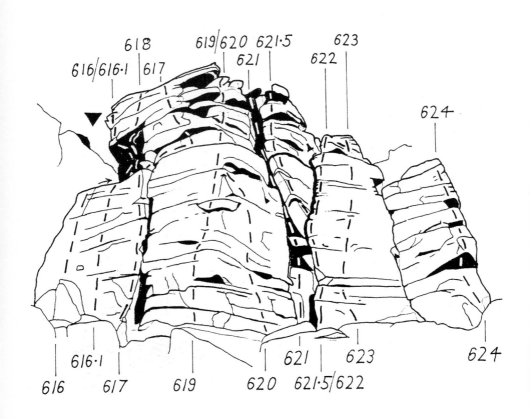

TWIN CHIMNEYS BUTTRESS

616	**Don't Bark, Bite**	18m	E1	5c	
616.1	**Rabies**	-	E1	5c	
617	**Crack and Cave**	18m	VD		
618	**Via Roof Route**	8m	VS	5a	
619	**Twin Chimneys Buttress**	17m	VS	4c	**
620	**Lucy's Delight**	15m	VS	4b	
621	**Left Twin Chimney**	15m	M	-	**
621.5	**Triplet**	17m	VS	4b	
622	**Right Twin Chimney**	11m	VD	-	**
623	**Bobsnob**	11m	E1	5a	
624	**Little John's Step**	21m	S	-	*

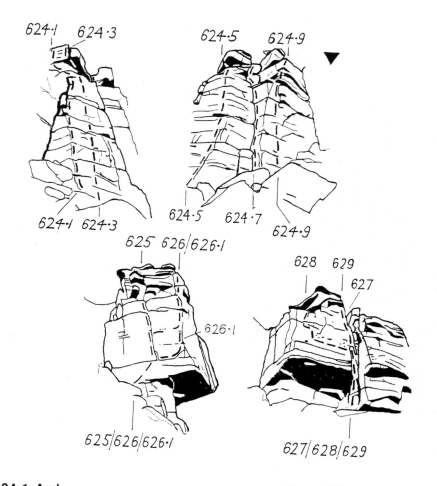

624.1	Awl	12m	VD		
624.3	Bean	15m	VS	5a	
624.5	Dun	15m	HS		
624.7	Bee	12m	HD		
624.9	Four	12m	VS	4c	
625	The Asp	8m	E3	6a	***
626	Boc No Buttress	18m	E5	6a	*
626.1	Direct Start	17m	E5	6c	*
627	R. Hood's Chockstone Chimney	17m	S	-	*
628	Wuthering	18m	E2	5b	***
629	Premier	18m	HVS	5a	

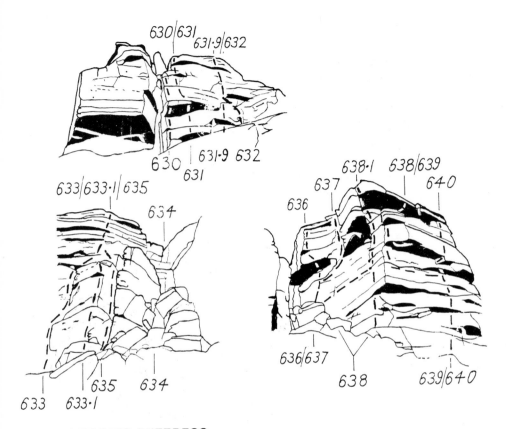

ROBIN HOOD'S BUTTRESS

630	Not Much Weak Stack Battered...	17m	E3	6b	
631	Withered Thing	17m	E2	6a	*
631.9	Wearing Thin	15m	E2	6a	
632	Paucity	15m	HVS	5b	*
633	Robin Hood's Crack	15m	VD		
633.1	Direct Start	-	VS	4c	
634	Robin Hood's Cave Gully	15m	D		
635	Tea-leaf Crack	15m	VD		
636	Last Ice Cream	12m	E2	5c	
637	Cave Gully Wall	12m	HVS	5a	**
638	Robin Hood's Cave Innominate	12m	VS	5a	**
638.1	Harding's Direct Finish	-	HVS	5a	
639	Last Bolt	13m	E3	5c	
640	Cave Eliminate	15m	E2	5c	**

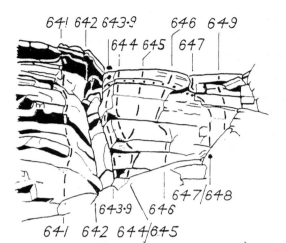

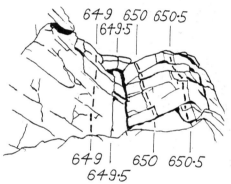

ROBIN HOOD'S BUTTRESS

641	Cave Arête	12m	HVS	5a	**
642	R. Hood's Balcony Cave Direct	12m	VD	-	*
643	Robin Hood's Cave Traverse	long	HVD		
	mid height 627-638				
643.9	Constipation Left Hand	12m	E2	5c	
644	Constipation	12m	E3	6a	*
645	Pacific Ocean Wall	12m	E5	6b	*
646	Desperation	12m	E1	5c	**
647	Robin Hood's Staircase	11m	VD		
648	Rubber Band (traverse)	20m	VS	4b	**
649	Kenneth	11m	VS	4b	
649.5	Stringer	10m	HS	4b	
650	Titbit	8m	VS	4c	
650.5	Meusli	11m	VS	5a	

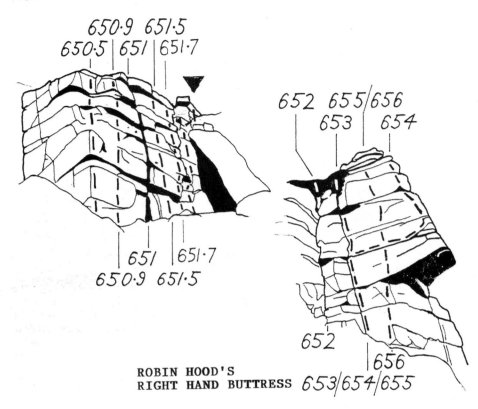

650·9 651·5
650·5 | 651 | 651·7

652 655/656
653 | 654

651 | 651·7
650·9 651·5

652

656
ROBIN HOOD'S
RIGHT HAND BUTTRESS 653/654/655

650.9	Cornflakes	11m	VS	5a	
651	Boot Crack	11m	HD		
651.5	Soft Shoe	10m	VS	5a	
651.7	Shuffle	10m	HS		
652	Twin Cracks	11m	D		
653	Right Twin Crack	11m	VS	4c	
654	Ellis's Eliminate	26m	VS	4c	**
655	Ginny Come Lately	12m	HVS	5b	*
656	Bob's Jolly Jape	12m	E3	6a	

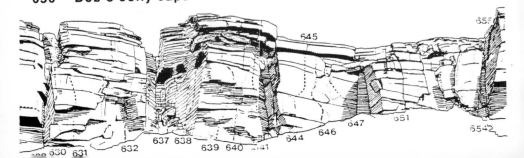

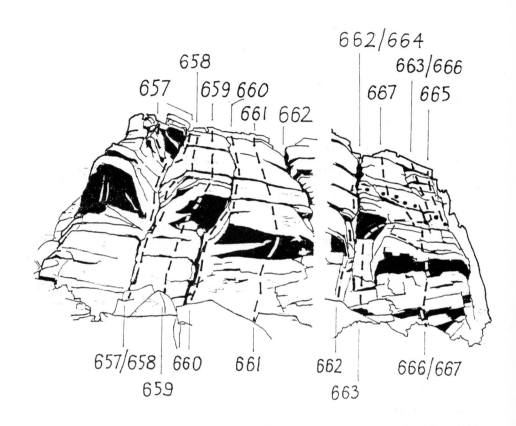

INVERTED V

657	Inverted V	21m	VS	4b	***
658	Retroversion	21m	HVS	4c	**
659	Our Version	21m	E3	6a	
660	Robin Hood RH Buttress Direct	23m	HS	-	***
661	Thunder Road	21m	E3	6a	*
662	Straight Crack	20m	VS	4c	
663	Robin Hood Zigzag	24m	S		
664	Bishop's Route traverse				
	mid height 668-662	24m	S		
665	Zagrete	18m	VS	4b	
666	Stage Fright	9m	E2	6a	
667	The Actress	9m	E1	5b	

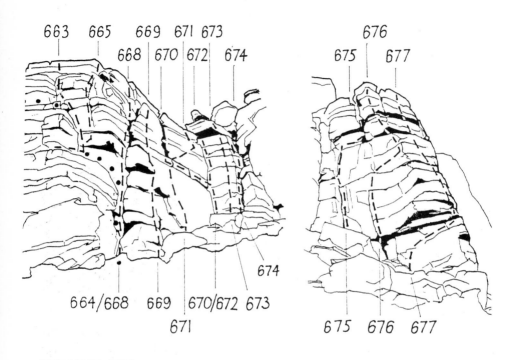

GREAT FLAKE

668	The Great Flake	18m	S	4a	*
669	Coconut Ice	18m	E2	5b	
670	The Little Flake	18m	VS	5a	
671	Ice Boat	20m	E1	5c	
672	Flake Chimney	15m	VD/S		
673	Hybrid	15m	HVS	5b	
674	Pedestal Chimney	15m	D		
675	Wright's Route	17m	VS	4c	
676	Wall of Sound	17m	E5	6b	***
677	Black Magic	16m	HVS	5b	**

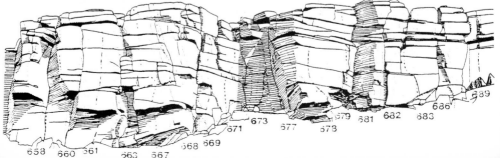

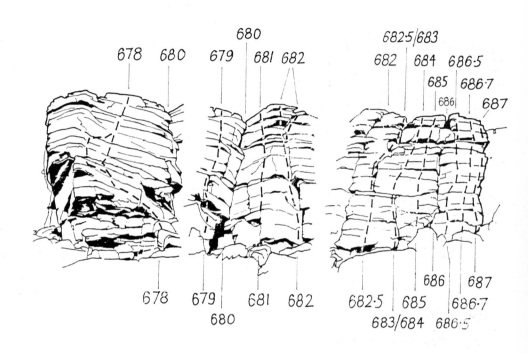

BLACK SLAB

678	Hargreaves' Original Route		
679	The Flange		
680	April Crack		
681	Easter Rib		
682	Christmas Crack		
682.5	Direct Start Central Trinity		
683	Central Trinity		
684	Twintrin		
685	Meiosis		
686	Right Hand Trinity		
686.5	Fergus Graham's Direct Route		
686.7	Well Right		
687	Topaz		

TRINITY WALL

16m	VS	4c	***
15m	HVS	5b	*
15m	HS	4b	**
15m	E1	5b	*
15m	HS	4b	***
-	HVS	5b	
15m	VS	4c	**
14m	E1	5c	
14m	HVS	5b	
13m	HS	4b	*
13m	VS	4c	
13m	E2	5c	
10m	E4	6a	

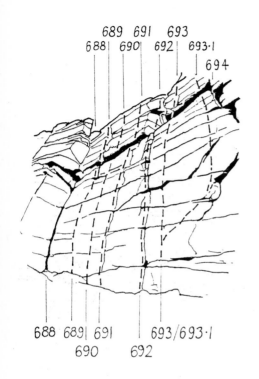
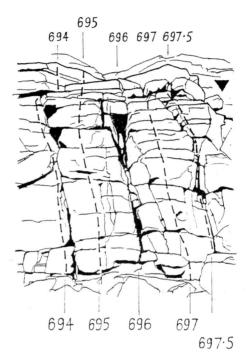

RUSTY WALL

688	Green Crack	11m	VS	4b	
689	Rugosity Wall	11m	HVS	5c	*
690	Rusty Wall	11m	HVS	6a	*
691	Rusty Crack	11m	HVS	5b	*
692	Via Media	11m	VS	4c	*
693	Via Dexter	11m	E2	5c	
693.1	Via Dexter Variation	11m	HVS	5a	
694	Oblique Crack	11m	S		
695	Oblique Buttress	11m	VS	5b	
696	Straight Chimney	11m	VD		
697	Albert's Pillar	11m	HS	4c	
697.5	Albert's Amble	11m	HVD		

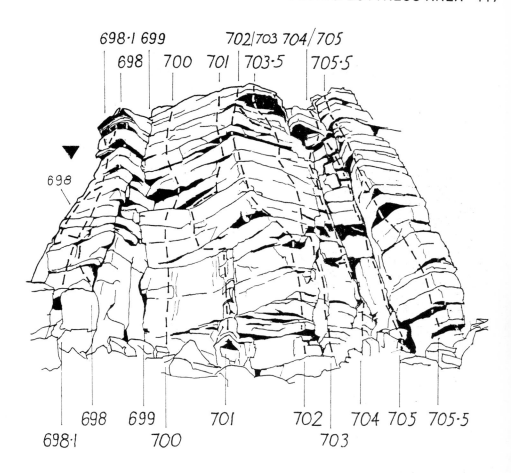

NARROW BUTTRESS

698	Narrow Buttress	14m	VS	4c	**
698.1	Straight and Narrow	14m	HVS	5a	
699	Hollybush Crack	14m	VD	-	***
700	Straightsville	15m	E2	5b	
701	Queersville	15m	HVS	5a	*
702	The Nose	15m	E3	6a	
703	Yosemite Wall	16m	E2	5b	*
703.5	El Cap Finish	-	E1	5b	
704	Leaning Butress Gully	15m	VS	4c	
705	Hangover	16m	VS	4c	
705.5	The Old Bag's Head	16m	E4	6a	

LEANING BUTTRESS

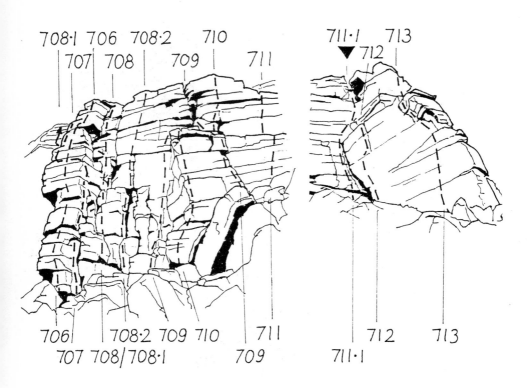

LEANING BUTTRESS

706	Leaning Buttress Direct	16m	HVS	5b	*
707	Leaning Buttress Indirect	16m	VD	-	*
708	Leaning Buttress Crack	15m	VD	-	*
708.1	The Bishop's Move	18m	VD		
708.2	That Sad Man	14m	E2	5c	
709	Garden Wall	14m	HVD		
710	Space Junk	14m	HVS	5b	
711	Birch Tree Wall	13m	HS	4b	
711.1	Scrappy Corner Descent	13m	-		
712	Mini Micro	6m	E2	6b	
713	Little Sarah	8m	HVS	5b	

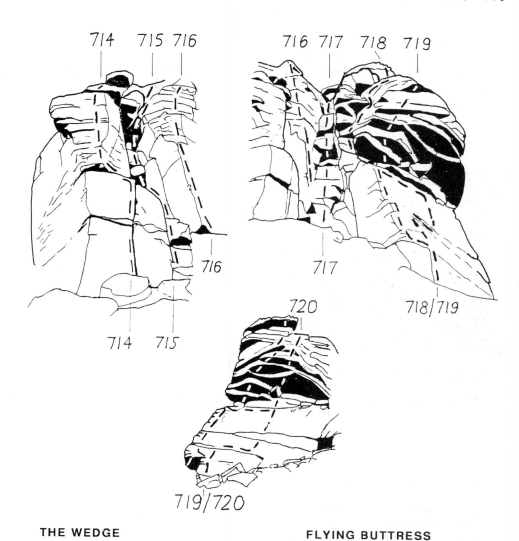

THE WEDGE

714	The Wedge	14m	VS	5a
715	Wedge Gully	12m	VS	4c
716	Wedge Rib	14m	VS	5a

FLYING BUTTRESS

717	Flying Buttress Gully	16m	D		
718	Flying Buttress	20m	VD	-	***
719	Goodbye Toulouse	18m	E1	5b	*
720	Flying Buttress Direct	16m	HVS	5b	***

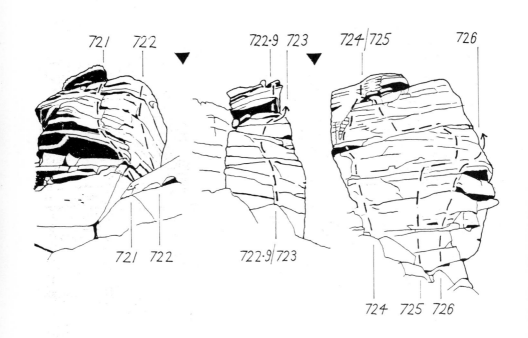

FLYING BUTTRESS

GREY WALL

721	**Kirkus's Corner**	14m	E1	5b	
722	**Spasticus Artisticus**	13m	E3	5c	
722.9	**Malarête**	12m	VS	4c	
723	**Jitterbug Buttress**	12m	S	4a	
724	**The Kirkus Original**	12m	VS	4c	
725	**Jitter Face**	13m	VD	-	*
726	**Townsend's Variation**	13m	HVS	4c	*

727	Censor	15m	E3	5c	*
728	Anxiety Attack	15m	E3	5c	
729	The Unprintable	16m	E1	5b	**
730	The Dangler	16m	E2	5c	**
731	Tippler Direct	16m	E3	6a	***
732	Paranoid	17m	E5	6b	*
733	The Tippler	20m	E1	5b	***

TIPPLER BUTTRESS

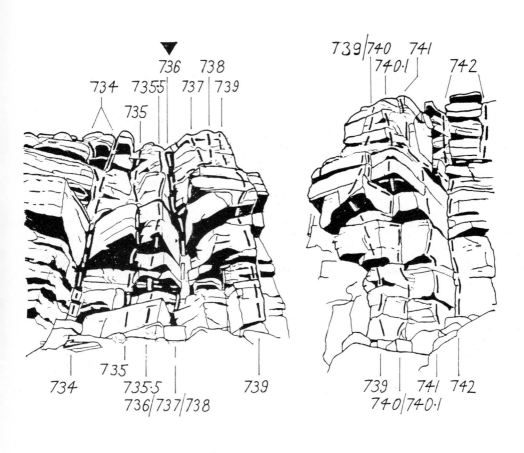

TIPPLER BUTTRESS

BLACK HAWK BUTTRESS

734	The Y Crack	18m	VS	4b	
735	The Z Crack	18m	VS	4c	
735.1	The Go Player	8m	E4	6b	
736	Castle (Black Hawk) Chimney	20m	M		
737	The Famous Ed Wood	20m	E1	5b	
738	Black Hawk Tower	21m	VD		
739	Chameleon	16m	E3	6a	**
740	Black Hawk Bastion	16m	E3	5c	**
740.1	Black Adder's Fortress	-	E4	6a	
741	Eliminator	15m	HVS	5b	*
742	Castle Crack (Black Hawk Slit)	18m	HS	4a	**

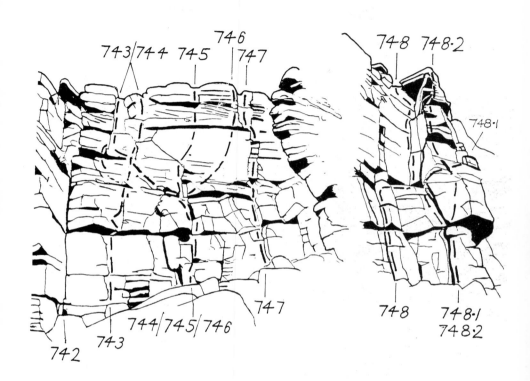

BLACK HAWK BUTTRESS

743	Black Hawk	15m	HS		
744	Black Hawk Traverse	17m	VD	-	*
744.1	Burgess's Variation	-	S		
745	Providence	15m	E1	5c	
746	Tribute to Kitty	15m	E5	6b	
747	Black Hawk Hell Crack	14m	S		**
748	Blizzard Chimney	16m	D	-	*
748.1	Gargoyle Variant	-	S		
748.2	Moriarty	16m	E3	6a	

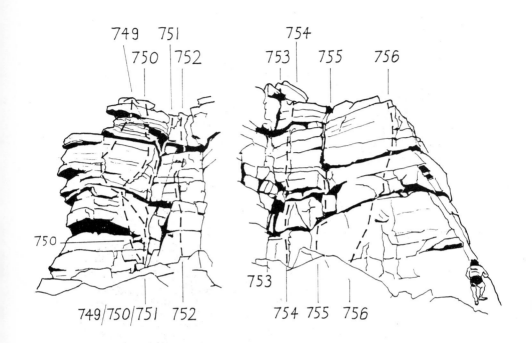

GARGOYLE BUTTRESS

749	Gargoyle Buttress	14m	VS	4b	*
750	Dry Rot	13m	E1	5b	
751	Physiology	13m	VD		
752	Sociology	13m	S		
753	Anatomy	13m	VD		
754	Tinker's Crack	13m	VS	4b	
755	Beggar's Crack	13m	VS	4c	
756	Tip Off	14m	E1	5b	

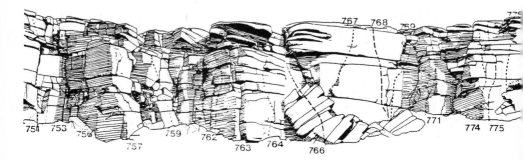

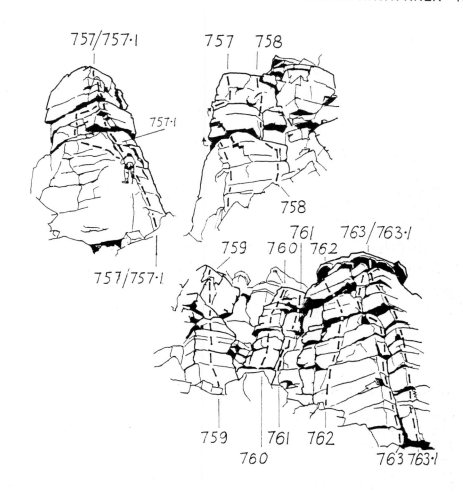

MANCHESTER BUTTRESS

757	**Manchester Buttress**	15m	HS	4b	**
757.1	**Manchester United**	-	HVS	5b	
758	**Tier Climb**	9m	VD		
759	**Two Tier Climb**	8m	VD		
760	**Cakestand**	9m	VD		
761	**Cool Groove**	10m	S		
762	**Lancashire Wall**	12m	HVS	5a	
763	**Crack and Corner**	15m	HVD	4b	***
763.1	**War Zone**	-	HVS	5c	

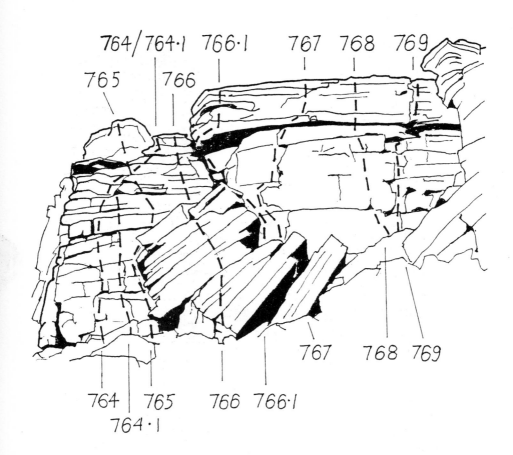

GROTTO SLAB

764	Heather Wall	12m	VS	4c	**
764.1	Heather Wall Variation	12m	HVS	5a	
765	Chimp's Corner	12m	VS	5a	
766	Grotto Slab	18m	D		
766.1	Jersey Boys	15m	E1	5a	
767	Grotto Wall	11m	HVS	4c	*
768	Reagent	11m	E5	6a	
769	Green Wall	10m	VS	4b	

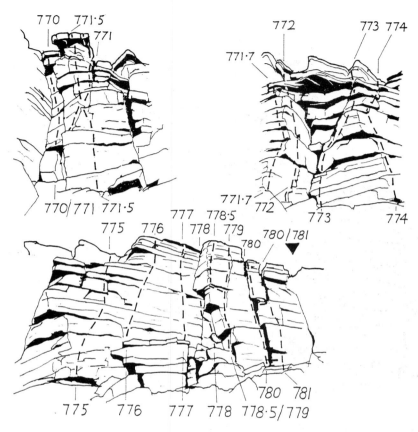

770	Capstone Chimney	8m	D	
771	Little Ernie	8m	S	
771.5	Big Chris	12m	E1	5b
771.7	In Earnest	10m	E1	5b
772	Recess Wall	10m	HVD	
773	Right Wall Route	10m	HVD	
774	Randolf Cheerleader	10m	E3	6a
775	Gullible's Travels	10m	E1	5b
776	Al	8m	E4	5c
777	The 3-D Wall	8m	E2	6a
778	Black Chimney	9m	M	
778.5	South Sea Charmer	9m	HVS	5b
779	Rugosity Crack	9m	HVS	5b	*
780	The Christiana Swing	10m	HVD	
781	Nicheless Climb	9m	S	

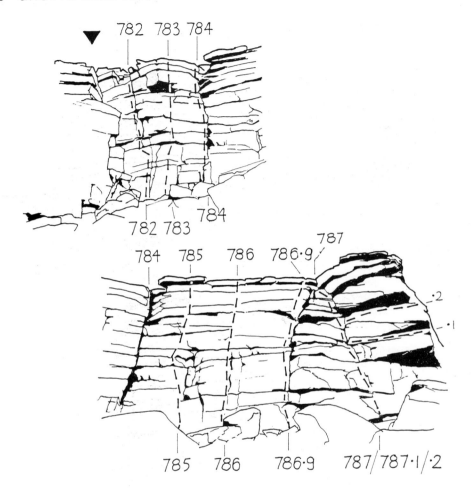

PLATE GLASS SLAB

MANTELPIECE BUTTRESS

782	Hoaxer's Crack	7m	S
783	Trivial Pursuit	6m	S
784	Small Crack	6m	D
785	Ground Glass	6m	VS	4c
786	Plate Glass Slab	6m	S
786.9	Mantelpiece Crack	7m	M
787	Mantelpiece Buttress	8m	D
787.1	Mantelpiece Hand-traverse lower	10m	HVS	4c
787.2	Mantelpiece Hand-traverse upper	10m	HVS	5a

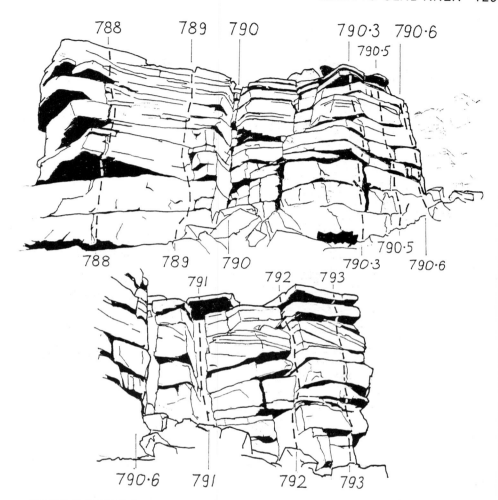

MANTELPIECE BUTTRESS

788	Mantelpiece Buttress Direct	8m	HVS	5a
789	Mantelpiece Right	7m	D	
790	Zip Crack	6m	M	
790.3	Button Wall	6m	VD	
790.5	Toggle	6m	VS	4b
790.6	Velcro Arête	6m	VD	
791	Square Chimney	6m	M	
792	Monkey Crack	6m	D	
793	Square Buttress Direct	7m	VS	5a

SQUARE BUTTRESS

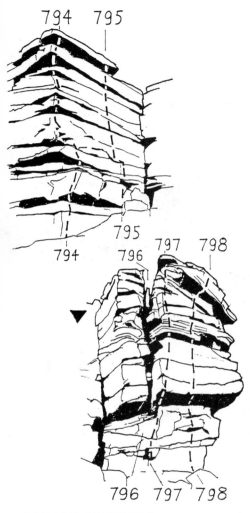

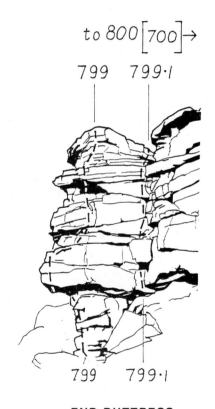

to 800 [700] →

SQUARE BUTTRESS

END BUTTRESS

794	**Square Buttress Arête**	6m	VS	4c
795	**Square Buttress Wall**	6m	S	4a
796	**Gashed Crack**	7m	VS	5a
797	**Ding Dong**	8m	VS	5b
798	**Suzanne**	8m	HVS	6a	*
799	**Finale**	8m	HVS	6a
799.1	**Fire Curtain**	8m	VD

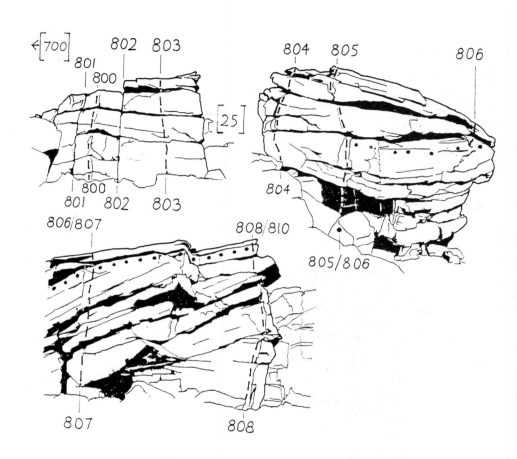

APPARENT NORTH BUTTRESS

800	Trainer Failure	6m	VS	5a	
801	Easy Jamming	6m	HVD		
802	The Real 20-foot Crack	20ft	VS	4c	
803	Twin Cam	6m	E4	6c	*
804	Frigid Witch	6m	HVS	5b	
805	Eminence Grise	7m	E1	5c	
806	Apparent North	10m	HVS	5b	**
807	Stanage Without Oxygen	9m	E5	6c	*
808	Magnetic North	9m	HVS	5c	

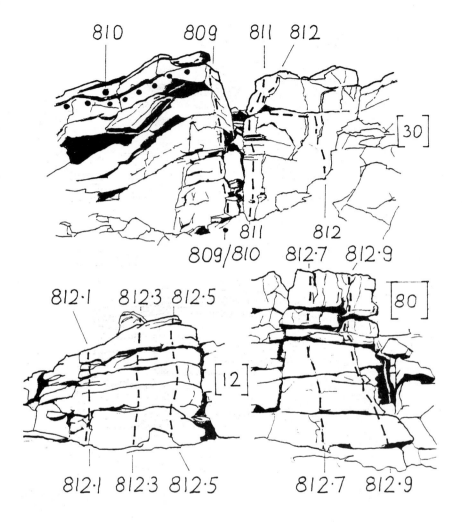

809	**True North**	9m	VS	4c
810	**Led a Dance** (traverse 806-809)	18m	HVS	5b
811	**Mating Toads**	6m	HVS	5c
812	**Massacre**	7m	HVS	5b
812.1	**Eeny**	5m	S	
812.3	**Meeny**	5m	HS	
812.5	**Miny**	5m	S	
812.7	**Spare Rib**	5m	VD	
812.9	**Scrag End**	5m	VD	

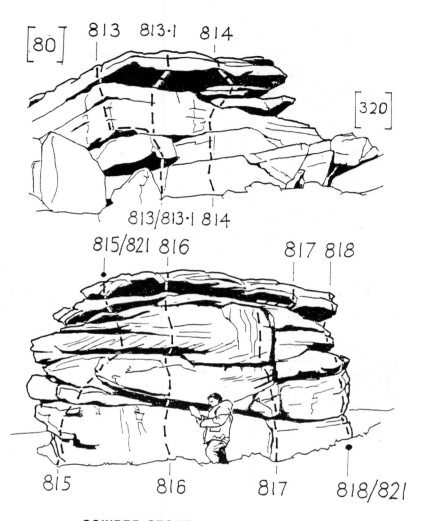

[80]
813   813·1   814

[320]

813/813·1 814

815/821 816   817 818

815   816   817   818/821

COWPER STONE

813	Petty Larceny	5m	HVS	5c	
813.1	Body Roll Finish	5m	E3	6a	
814	Grand Theft	6m	HVS	5c	*
815	Whatever Happened to Bob?	7m	E2	5c	
816	Sad Among Friends	8m	E6	6c	**
817	Snug as a Thug on a Jug	8m	E4	6b	**
818	Breakdance	7m	E3	6a	

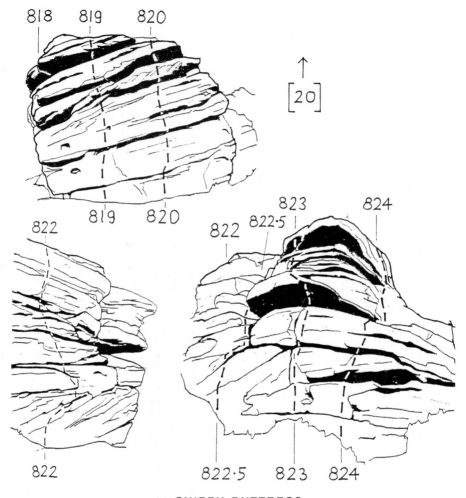

CHIPPY BUTTRESS

819	Leroy Slips a Disc	6m	E2	6c	
820	Head Spin	6m	E1	6a	
821	Traverse of the Gritstone				
	Gods (818 - 815)	14m	E4	6b	**
822	Pudding	7m	E1	5c	
822.5	Salt and Vinegar	6m	S		
823	Chips	7m	E3	5c	
824	Peas	11m	E4	5c	

INDEX

21 Today	HVS	34
3-D Wall, The	E2	127
49 Bikinis	HVS	100
49th Parallel	HS	46
5.9 Finish	E1	95
7% Soln	HVS	23
* A Day Without Pay	E6	72
A Problem of Coagulation	E3	85
A Thousand Natural Shocks	HVS	62
Abacus	E2	55
Accessory Chimney	D	94
* Acheron	E1	103
Actress, The	E1	113
Acute Amnesia	HVS	23
Additive Chimney	VD	73
Adult Only	E1	70
Aeneid, The	VS	103
African Herbs	E2	104
Afterthought	HVD	61
** Agony Crack	HVS	107
Al	E4	127
Albert's Amble	HVD	116
Albert's Pillar	HS	116
Amazing Harry Greystoke II, The	VS	59
* Amazon Crack	S	105
American Gritfeati	HVS	84
Ami	M	42
Amoeba on the Edge of Time	VS	57
Amphitheatre Face	VS	63
Anatomy	VD	124
Angus	VD	45
Anji	VS	76
** Anniversary Arête	E1	46
Another Turn	S	20
Anxiety Attack 2	E2	56
Anxiety Attack	E3	121
** Apparent North	HVS	131
** April Crack	HS	115
*** Archangel	E3	68
* Argus	E2	63
* Ariel, The	VD	20
* Aries	S	36
Arrow Crack	VS	24
Arsenic Poisoning	HVS	51
* Ashes	E3	102
*** Asp, The	E3	109
August Arête	HVS	89
Autumn Gold	HS	30
* Avril	S	23
Awl	VD	109
B Crack	D	56
Back Door	VS	28
** Back in the Y.M.C.A.	E4	85
Back to School	HVS	82
Bad Do	HVS	20
Badly Bitten	E4	88
Balance	D	24
*** Balcony Buttress	S	106
Balcony Climb	HVD	106
Balcony Corner	D	106
Balcony Cracks	S	106
Bandits in the Woods	VS	32
Basil Brush	HVS	56
Basil Half-tail	E1	60
Bastille	E1	63
Bath Oil	HS	19
Bathtime for Two	HS	19
*** BAW's Crawl	HVS	96
Beads	S	100
Beady Eye	VS	94
Beaky	VS	53
Bean	VS	109
Beanpod	S	34
* Beautician, The	E3	39
Bee	HD	109
Beggar's Crack	VS	124
* Bent Crack	HD	30
Between the Two	HVS	86
Bifurcated Headplate Max	VS	27
Big Air	E6	70
Big Al	HVS	30
Big Bob's Bazzer	HVS	81
Big C, The	VS	52
Big Chris	E1	127
* Big Screams	E1	79
Big Yin	VS	106
** Billiard Buttress	HVS	85
Birch Tree Wall	HS	118
Birthday Buttress	HS	34
Bishop's Move, The	VD	118
Bishop's Route	S	113
Black Adder's Fortress	E4	122
Black and Decker	E1	59
Black Attack	E3	51
Black Chimney	M	127
Black Hawk	HS	123
** Black Hawk Bastion	E3	122
** Black Hawk Hell Crack	S	123
Black Hawk Tower	VD	122
* Black Hawk Traverse	VD	123
** Black Magic	HVS	114
Blinkers	VS	24
* Blizzard Chimney	D	123
* Blockhead Direct	HVS	45
Bloodshot	E3	101
Blow Out	HVS	49
Blue Fluff	E4	87
** Blurter, The	HVS	36

	Bob's Jolly Jape	E3	112
	Bobsnob	E1	108
*	Boc No Buttress	E5	109
	Body Roll Finish	E3	133
	Bolt Buttress	VS	50
	Bon Ami	VS	57
	Boobagram	E1	60
	Boomerang Chimney	VD	24
	Boot Crack	HD	112
	Boris the Bold	VS	107
	Bottomless Crack	HVS	31
*	Bow Crack	HD	31
	Boyd's Crack	M	41
**	Boys Will Be Boys	E6	88
*	Breadline	E4	70
	Breakdance	E3	133
	Bright Eyed	VS	30
	Brittle Bones	E1	26
*	Broken Buttress	D	48
	Broken Groove	VD	48
	Broken In	HS	48
	Brushed	E2	70
	Bumblies in Red Socks	E3	89
	Burgess Crack	D	48
	Burgess's Variation	S	123
	Butcher Crack	HVS	98
	Button Wall	VD	129
	Byne's Route	S	101
	Cakestand	VD	125
	Caliban's Cave	S	21
*	Calluna	M	43
**	Calvary	E4	90
	Calvary Direct	E5	90
	Cannon	D	86
	Canton	D	58
	Capstone Chimney (3-D Wall)	D	127
	Capstone Chimney (Wall Buttress)	D	88
**	Careless Torque	E6	70
	Castle (Black Hawk) Chimney	M	122
**	Castle Crack (Black Hawk Slit)	HS	122
**	Cave Arête	HVS	111
	Cave Buttress	VD	42
**	Cave Eliminate	E2	110
**	Cave Gully Wall	HVS	110
*	Censor	E3	121
	Cent	E1	41
*	Centaur	E1	73
*	Central Buttress	VS	50
*	Central Buttress Direct	E1	50
	Central Chimney	M	50
**	Central Trinity	VS	115
	Centrepiece	VS	50
*	Centurion's Slab	M	53
	Certainly Parakeratosis	HVS	31
**	Chameleon	E3	122
	Cheapest Topping	VS	78
	Cheeky Little Number	E1	33
	Cheque	VD	66
	Child's Play	HVS	21
	Chimp's Corner	VS	126
*	Chip Shop Brawl	E5	21
	Chips	E3	134
	Chockstone Chimney	M	91
	Chockstone Crack	D	92
	Choux	E2	101
	Choux Fleur	E1	101
	Christiana Swing, The	HVD	127
***	Christmas Crack	HS	115
	Chute, The	S	76
*	Cinturato	E1	73
	Cleft Wall Route 1	VD	91
	Cleft Wall Route 2	S	91
	Cleft Wing	VS	95
	Cleft Wing Superdirect	VS	95
	Clegg	HVD	43
	Clubbing	E3	26
	Cocktail	VS	99
	Coconut Ice	E2	114
	Coign, The	S	66
	Comet	E3	84
	Compost Corner	D	77
*	Comus	E4	84
*	Concept of Kinky	E5	23
	Confectioner, The	VS	99
***	Congo Corner	HVS	104
*	Constipation	E3	111
	Constipation Left Hand	E2	111
*	Cool Curl, The	E6	55
	Cool Groove	S	125
	Corduroy	VS	72
	Corner Crack	HS	81
	Corner Crack	VD	46
	Cornflakes	VS	112
**	Cosmic Crack	VS	34
	Count Me Out	E2	55
*	Count's Buttress	E1	55
	Count's Buttress Direct	E2	55
*	Count's Chimney	D	55
**	Count's Crack	VS	56
	Count's Wall	HVS	55
*	Count, The	E1	55
	Counterblast	E2	55
	Countess Buttress	VS	50
*	Crab Crawl Arête	VS	21
*	Crab Crawl, The	S	21
	Crack and Cave	VD	108
***	Crack and Corner	HVD	125
	Cracked Wall	HVD	47
	Cracked Wall Direct	VS	47
	Crawly	VD	47
	Creepy	S	47

	Creepy Crawly	HS	47
	Crescent	VS	76
**	Crescent Arête	HVS	70
*	Crew Pegs Diffs	E3	35
**	Crime	E3	83
	Cringe	VS	47
	Cripple's Crack	HVD	22
	Crossover	E2	83
	Crumbling Crack	HS	25
***	Crypt Trip,The	E5	41
**	Cue	HVS	85
*	Curved Crack	VD	85
*	Curving Buttress	E2	92
	Curving Buttress Corner	M	92
**	Curving Chimney	D	92
	Curving Chimney Left Arête	E2	92
**	D.I.Y.	E3	59
	Daboecia	M	43
	Dalesman, The	HVS	41
**	Dangler, The	E2	121
	Dark Angel	HVS	68
**	Dark Continent	E1	104
	Dark Water	E3	103
*	Daydreamer	E2	54
	Death and Night and Blood	E1	67
	Deep Chimney	D	35
**	Defying Destiny	E5	90
	Defying Destiny Direct	-	90
	Delicious	VD	92
	Delightful	M	92
	Delirious	D	93
	Deliverance, The	-	83
	Delovely	HS	93
**	Desperation	E1	111
**	Deuteronomy	HVS	33
**	Devil's Chimney	D	102
	Dieppe	VS	94
	Dijon Dip	E2	64
	Ding Dong	VS	130
**	Direct Loss	E4	88
	Direct Start Central Trinity	HVS	115
	Dissuader	HS	48
*	Doctor's Chimney	VD	22
	Doctored	HVS	22
	Don	E4	68
	Don's Delight	HVS	27
	Don't Bark, Bite	E1	108
	Doncaster's Route	HVS	68
	Dot's Slab	D	60
	Double Act	HVS	69
	Dover's Wall Route 3	VS	94
	Dover's Wall, Route 1	HVD	95
	Dover's Wall, Route 2	HVS	95
	Dover's Wall, Route 4	VS	95
	Dracula	HVS	56
	Dream Boat	E3	54
	Dry Crack	D	60
	Dry Rot	E1	124
	Duchess	HVS	53
	Dun	HS	109
	Duo Crack Climb	D	37
	E.M.F.	VS	33
	Early Starter	E1	91
*	Easter Rib	E1	115
	Easy Jamming	HVD	131
	Eckhard's Arête	S	40
	Eckhard's Chimney	VD	40
	Edale Trip (Beyond Hope)	E3	80
	Eden Arête	S	54
	Editor's Vaseline	HVS	89
	Eeny	S	132
	El Cap Finish	E1	117
	Electron	VS	34
	Elephant in the Doghouse	E1	86
*	Eliminator	HVS	122
**	Ellis's Eliminate	VS	112
	Eminence Grise	E1	131
	Enclosure Crack	D	50
*	Eric's Eliminate	S	39
	Erica	M	43
	Erica Micra	HS	35
	Esso Extra	E1	73
	Europa	E4	51
**	Exaltation	E5	23
*	Exodus	HVS	33
	Eyes	VS	96
*	Fading Star	E2	102
	Fading Star direct start	-	102
	Fairy Castle Crack	D	105
	Fairy Chimney	D	105
**	Fairy Steps	VS	69
	Fallen Pillar Chimney	VD	105
	Famous Ed Wood, The	E1	122
	Faster	VS	19
*	Fate	HVS	37
	Fear and Loathing	E3	89
	Feathered Friends	VS	29
*	February Crack	HS	23
	Feminist's Breakfast	E4	61
	Fergus Graham's Direct Route	VS	115
**	Fern Crack	VS	64
**	Fern Groove	E2	64
	Ferryboat Highway	HVS	105
*	Fina	HVS	72
	Finale	HVS	130
	Fire Curtain	VD	130
*	First Sister	VS	28
	Flake Chimney	VD/S	114
	Flake Gully	M	82
	Flaked Crack	HVD	57
	Flaked Traverse	HVD	57
	Flaky Wall	HVS	63

* Flange, The	HVS	115
Flate	VS	83
Flesh and Blood	VS	26
Flipside	E2	35
Flue, The	VD	106
Flute Chimney	D	60
*** Flying Buttress	VD	119
*** Flying Buttress Direct	HVS	119
Flying Buttress Gully	D	119
Foetus on the Eiger	E1	76
Four	VS	109
Four Star	E3	72
Four Winds; Eight Directions	E3	51
Freeze	HVS	38
Frigid Witch	HVS	131
Frosty	D	38
Fulcrum	HVS	81
Gameo	E2	23
Garden Wall	HVD	118
Gardener's Crack	D	78
Gardener's Groove	HS	77
* Gargoyle Buttress	VS	124
Gargoyle Variant	S	123
Gashed Crack	VS	130
Gathering Gloom	E1	103
Genesis	VS	46
* Germ	E2	25
* Ginny Come Lately	HVS	112
Giro	E2	66
Gnat's Slab	M	44
Gnat's Slab Arête	S	44
Gnome Direct Start	-	69
Gnome Man's Land	E4	69
Go Player, The	E4	122
*** Goliath's Groove	HVS	68
* Good Clean Fun	E4	23
* Goodbye Toulouse	E1	119
*** Goosey Goosey Gander	E4	27
** Grace and Danger	E6	73
Graduate, The	E1	50
* Grain of Truth	E3	46
* Grand Theft	HVS	133
* Great Flake, The	S	114
Green Crack	VD	27
Green Crack	VS	116
Green Line	HVS	28
Green Needle Gully descent	-	107
Green Party	VS	20
** Green Streak, The	HVS	20
Green Wall	VS	126
* Greengrocer Wall	HVS	99
Grime	HS	59
Gripe Fruit Juice	HVS	80
Grooved Arête	S	76
Grope Slope	E1	96
Groper, The	VS	94
Grotto Slab	D	126
* Grotto Wall	HVS	126
Ground Glass	VS	128
*** Guillotine Direct	E4	98
** Guillotine, The	E3	98
Gullible's Travels	E1	127
Gunter	VS	39
Hairless Art	HVS	59
Hangover	VS	117
Harding's Direct Finish	HVS	110
Hardly Hyperkeratosis	E2	31
*** Hargreaves' Original Route	VS	115
** Harvest	E3	27
** Hathersage Trip, The	E4	81
Have a Break	E3	58
Have a Nice Day	VS	58
Haze	HVS	50
Head Over Heels	E3	51
Head Spin	E1	134
* Headbanger	E1	45
* Hearsay Crack	HVS	35
* Heath Robinson	E5	22
Heather Crack	HVD	35
Heather Slab	D	49
** Heather Wall	VS	126
Heather Wall Variation	HVS	126
Heaven Crack	VD	103
* Helfenstein's Struggle	D	68
** Hell Crack	VS	103
Help the Aged (direct start)	-	64
Help the Aged	E2	64
Hercules Crack	VD	80
Hidden Crack	VD	97
* High and Wild	E3	42
* High Flyer	E4	21
*** High Neb Buttress	VS	41
High Neb Edge	HVS	41
** High Neb Girdle Traverse	S	42
High Neb Gully	-	41
High Tide	VS	52
Hoaxer's Crack	S	128
Holly Crack	VD	89
*** Hollybush Crack	VD	117
Hollybush Gully Left	S	69
Hollybush Gully Right	M	69
Horn	VS	82
* Hot and Bothered	E3	73
Hot Spur	VS	71
Hybrid	HVS	114
I Didn't Get Where I am Today	E2	62
I Never Said It Was Any Good	E1	68
Ice Boat	E1	114
Ice Cream Flakes	VD	38
Icy Crack	VS	38
** Impossible Slab	E2	40
* Improbability Drive	E3	88

*	In a Big Way Yerself	E4	28
	In Earnest	E1	127
**	In-off	E3	85
*	Inaccessible Crack	VS	39
	Inaccessible Slab	S	39
*	Incursion	E1	20
*	Incursion Direct	E1	20
**	Indian Summer	E5	75
	Insomniac	E1	54
	Intermediate Buttress	VD	100
	Introvert, The	E2	62
***	Inverted V	VS	113
	Jam Good	VD	33
	Jammed Stone Chimney	VD	65
	Jammy	HD	92
	Jean's Line	VS	103
	Jean's Route	VS	36
*	Jeepers Creepers	HVS	42
	Jersey Boys	E1	126
	Jim Crow	VS	29
*	Jitter Face	VD	120
	Jitterbug Buttress	S	120
	Jon's Route	VS	96
	Kangaroo	VS	94
	Keep Pedalling	E2	97
	Keith's Crack	HS	51
	Kelly's Crack	D	29
*	Kelly's Eliminate	D	29
	Kelly's Eye	S	29
**	Kelly's Overhang	HVS	39
	Kelly's Variation	VD	40
	Kenneth	VS	111
	Kerb	HD	21
	Kindergarten	VS	21
*	King Kong	E3	40
	Kirkus Original, The	VS	120
	Kirkus's Corner	E1	120
	Kitcat	VS	58
	Kitten	VS	33
*	Knutter, The	HVS	35
	Ladder Corner	M	63
	Ladder Cracks	D	63
**	Lamia, The	E2	27
	Lancashire Wall	HVS	125
	Last Bolt	E3	110
	Last Ice Cream	E2	110
	Leaning Buttress Gully	VS	117
*	Leaning Buttress Crack	VD	118
*	Leaning Buttress Direct	HVS	118
*	Leaning Buttress Indirect	VD	118
	Leaps and Bounds	E1	69
	Led a Dance	HVS	132
	Left	VD	46
	Left Hand Tower	VS	28
	Left Over	VS	65
	Left Pool Crack	D	86
	Left Spur	-	71
**	Left Twin Chimney	M	108
***	Left Unconquerable, The	E1	91
	Lepton	HS	32
	Leroy Slips a Disc	E2	134
	Lethe	HVS	103
	Letter-box	D	51
	Levee, The	HVS	104
*	Leviticus	HVS	33
	Life Begins at 40	HVS	34
	Limbo	S	41
***	Link, The	HVS	104
	Lino	VD	56
	Little Ernie	S	127
	Little Flake, The	VS	114
*	Little John's Step	S	108
	Little Sarah	HVS	118
	Little Slab	D	42
	Little Things	VS	34
	Little Tower	HS	100
*	Little Unconquerable, The	HVS	91
	Living at the Speed	E1	72
*	Logic Book, The	E2	40
	Lonely Crag	D	26
	Look Before You Leap	E1	62
	Lookout Flake	S	62
	Lost Count	HVS	56
	Lost Soul	S	41
	Louis the Loon	E2	72
*	Louisiana Rib, The	VS	103
	Love Handles	HVS	25
	Lucky Strike	E1	91
	Lucy's Delight	VS	108
	Lucy's Slab	HVS	36
	Lusitania	S	44
	Lusitania Direct Finish	HS	44
	Lysteria Hysteria	E3	31
	M Route	VS	107
	Ma's Retreat	HVS	60
	Magazine	VS	46
	Magnetic North	HVS	131
	Mai	VS	23
	Malarête	VS	120
**	Manchester Buttress	HS	125
	Manchester United	HVS	125
	Mangler, The	E1	76
	Manhattan Arête	D	22
	Manhattan Chimney	D	22
	Manhattan Crack	VS	22
	Mantelpiece	VS	50
	Mantelpiece Buttress	D	128
	Mantelpiece Buttress Direct	HVS	129
	Mantelpiece Crack	M	128
	Mantelpiece Hand-traverse lower	HVS	128
	Mantelpiece Hand-traverse upper	HVS	128
	Mantelpiece Right	D	129

Mantelshelf Climb	D	42	
* Marble Arête	HS	27	
Marble Tower Flake	VD	27	
Margery Daw	HVS	81	
Marie Celeste	E1	44	
Mark Devalued	VS	72	
Mark's Slab	VS	72	
Marmalade's Lost Start	E1	92	
Marmite	HS	59	
Marmoset, The	HS	30	
Mars	VD	23	
Martello Buttress	HS	101	
Martello Cracks	M	102	
Mary Whitehouse	-	98	
Massacre	HVS	132	
Mate	E1	66	
Mating Toads	HVS	132	
May Crack	VS	30	
Me	HVS	19	
Meddle	E2	36	
Meeny	HS	132	
Meiosis	HVS	115	
Melancholy Witness	E3	105	
Memory Loss	HVS	88	
Meninblack II	E2	52	
Mercury Crack	VD	80	
Mersey Variant, The	E2	104	
Meson	VD	32	
Meusli	VS	111	
Michelle My Belle	E3	90	
* Microbe	HVS	25	
Midge	D	43	
Millsom's Direct	E3	85	
** Millsom's Minion	E1	85	
Milton's Meander	VS	84	
Mini Micro	E2	118	
Mini Motor Mile	VS	53	
Miny	S	132	
Miranda's Variation	VD	21	
Miserable Miracle	HVS	75	
Miss World	HS	45	
Missing Link	E2	26	
Missing Numbers	HVS	33	
*** Missisippi Buttress Direct	VS	104	
** Mississippi Chimney	VD	104	
* Mississippi Variant	E1	105	
Mistella	VD	102	
Mitch Pitch	HVS	86	
Modest Carpenter, The	E4	41	
Modesty	VS	86	
Monad	E1	24	
Monday Blue	E2	91	
Monkey Crack	D	129	
Moriarty	E3	123	
* Moribund	E3	88	
* Morrison's Redoubt	E1	105	
Mother's Day	VS	61	
Motor Mile	HVS	53	
Mounting Frustration	E2	94	
Mouthpiece	E2	39	
Move	HD	19	
Mr M'Quod and the Anti-rock Squad	HVS	25	
Mr Pemphigoid	HVS	26	
Mr Universe	E3	45	
My Herald of Free Enterprise	E6	81	
N Route	HS	107	
Nairobi	E4	104	
** Namenlos	E1	88	
Narlavision	HVS	65	
** Narrow Buttress	VS	117	
Narrowing Chimney	S	100	
Nasty Green Dwarf	VS	78	
National Breakdown	E3	81	
Naughtical Slab	VS	52	
Neb Corner	D	40	
*** Nectar	E4	27	
Nephron	VS	87	
Neutrons For Old	E2	76	
New Year's Eve	S	30	
New York, New York	E1	22	
Newhaven	VD	94	
Nice One	VD	46	
Niche Climb	S	22	
Niche Wall	VS	22	
Nicheless Climb	S	127	
* Nightmare Slab	E1	54	
Nightride Corner	VD	54	
Nightrider	E2	54	
* Nightsalt	E4	90	
Nihilistic Narl	E4	75	
No Man	HS	52	
*** No More Excuses	E4	35	
Non-stop Pedalling	E2	96	
Non-toxic	VS	60	
* Norse Corner Climb	HS	40	
Nose, The	E3	117	
* Nose, The	VS	100	
Not Much Weak Stack Battered..	E3	110	
Not Richard's Sister Direct	E1	28	
*** Not To Be Taken Away	E2	70	
Nothing to do with Dover	HVS	94	
Nuke the Midges	E1	75	
Nursery Crack	VS	21	
Oblique Buttress	VS	116	
Oblique Crack	S	116	
Obstinance	VS	77	
October Crack	D	30	
October Slab	S	30	
Of Old	S	94	
** Off With His Head	E4	98	
Old Bag's Head, The	E4	117	

	Old Dragon, The	E1	98
***	Old Friends	E4	41
**	Old Salt	HVS	23
*	Ono	S	37
**	Orang-outang	E1	27
	Original Scoop	VS	101
	Our Version	E3	113
	Out for the Count	E4	55
	Outlook Buttress	HVS	62
	Outlook Chimney	VS	62
	Outlook Crack	VS	62
	Outlook Layback	S	62
	Outlook Slab	VS	67
	Overcoat	HVS	36
	Overflow	E1	39
	Overhanging Chimney	VD	36
	Overhanging Crack	VS	81
*	Overhanging Wall	HVS	83
	P.O. Crack	HS	66
	Pacemaker	HVS	28
*	Pacific Ocean Wall	E5	111
	Pal	S	94
	Pal Joey	VD	94
	Palermo	VD	94
	Paping About...	VS	79
	Paradise Arête	VS	84
	Paradise Crack	D	84
	Paradise Lost	D	84
**	Paradise Wall	VS	84
	Parallel Cracks	VS	46
	Paralysis	VS	107
*	Paranoid	E5	121
	Parasite	HVS	84
	Passover	E2	83
*	Paucity	HVS	110
	Paved Vacuum	VS	21
	Peas	E4	134
	Pebble Arête	-	83
	Pedestal Chimney	D	114
	Pedlar's Arête	HVS	97
*	Pedlar's Rib	E1	96
*	Pedlar's Slab	HVS	97
*	Pegasus Rib	HVS	82
*	Pegasus Wall	VS	82
	Percy's Prow	S	78
	Perforation	HVS	29
	Persuader	VS	48
	Pertinacious	HVS	48
	Petty Larceny	HVS	133
*	Phlegethoa	HVS	102
	Photograph, The	E3	70
	Physician's Wall	E1	22
	Physiology	VD	124
*	Pig's Ear	E1	35
	Pillar Arête	VD	92
	Pinch	HS	92

*	Pinion, The	VD	20
*	Pisa Crack	HVD	97
	Pisa Pillar	HS	97
	Pixie	VS	105
	Pizza Slab	S	78
	Plastic Dream	E3	97
	Plate Glass Slab	S	128
	Plugging the Gap	HVS	91
	Pool Wall	VS	86
	Poor Pizza	D	78
**	Pot Black	E2	85
	Prairie Dog	HVS	45
	Premier	HVS	109
	Preston's Wall	HVS	58
	Pretty Petty	HVS	94
	Prickly Crack	VD	56
	Problem Corner	VS	25
	Problem Crack	-	25
*	Prospero's Climb	VD	21
	Protractor	HVS	58
	Providence	E1	123
	Prowler	HVS	49
	Public Image	VS	96
	Pudding	E1	134
*	Pullover	HVS	72
	Pulse	HVS	34
**	Punishment	E4	83
*	Punk, The	VS	96
*	Punklet	HVS	96
	Pup	HVS	33
	Pure Gossip	HS	35
	Pure, White and Deadly	E2	65
	Puss	HVS	33
*	Puzzlelock	E4	105
	QE2	VS	44
*	Quadrille	S	31
	Quantum Crack	VS	34
	Quartz	HVS	85
*	Queersville	HVS	117
***	Quietus	E2	40
*	Quietus Right-hand	E4	40
	Quiver	HVS	24
	Rabbit's Crack	VS	29
	Rabies	E1	108
	Rack, The	D	20
	Radox	S	33
	Randolf Cheerleader	E3	127
	Reagent	E5	126
	Real 20-foot Crack, The	VS	131
	Recess Rib	D	97
	Recess Wall	HVD	127
	Regret	E2	107
**	Retroversion	HVS	113
	Rib and Face	HVS	106
	Rib Chimney	D	90
	Richard's Sister	S	28

Ride Him Cowboy VS 71
Right HS 46
** Right Hand Tower HVS 28
* Right Hand Trinity HS 1·15
Right Pool Crack D 86
Right Spur - 71
** Right Twin Chimney VD 108
Right Twin Crack VS 112
*** Right Unconquerable, The HVS 91
Right Wall S 93
Right Wall Route HVD 127
Rigor Mortis HS 107
Rimmington Place E2 24
Rinty VS 37
Ritornel HVS 91
*** Robin Hood RH Buttress Direct HS 113
Robin Hood Zigzag S 113
* Robin Hood's Balcony Cave Direct VD 111
Robin Hood's Cave Gully D 110
** Robin Hood's Cave Innominate VS 110
Robin Hood's Cave Traverse HVD 111
* Robin Hood's Chockstone Chimney S 109
Robin Hood's Crack VD 110
Robin Hood's Staircase VD 111
Roll Neck VS 72
Rotor - 70
Roundabout, The HVS 100
** Rubber Band VS 111
* Rugosity Crack HVS 127
* Rugosity Wall HVS 116
* Rusty Crack HVS 116
* Rusty Wall HVS 116
** Sad Among Friends E6 133
* Saliva HVS 102
Salt and Vinegar S 134
* Saltation E4 23
Sand Crack S 85
Sand Gully D 84
* Satin E3 72
Savage Amusement E2 107
Scavenger VS 45
* Sceptic HVS 27
Scoop and Corner M 93
Scoop Crack VD 106
*** Scoop, The (Ozymandias) HVS 101
Scorpion Slab VD 79
Scrag End VD 132
Scraped Crack D 56
Scrappy Corner Descent - 118
Scraps VS 45
Scrole Not Dole E5 75
Scuppered E4 75
Second Sister VS 28
Second Wind HVS 100

* Seesaw VS 81
* Seranata E1 31
Setsquare HVD 58
Shaky Gully VD 63
Sharpener HVS 58
* Shelf Life E3 80
Shine On E7 96
*** Shirley's Shining Temple E5 56
* Shock Horror Slab E1 56
Short Crack M 60
Short Straw VS 89
Shuffle HS 112
Side Effect VS 32
Side Plate S 38
Sidelined E2 70
Sideslip E2 70
Silence HVS 40
** Silica E2 85
** Silk E5 64
Sinew Stretch HVS 45
Sinister VS 46
Sithee E1 59
* Skidoo E6 76
Skin Grafter E2 60
Slab and Crack VS 77
Slanting Chimney S 66
Slanting Chimney VD 51
Slanting Crack HS 87
* Slap 'n' Spittle E4 28
Sleepwalker HVS 54
Slight Second E1 20
Slow Down S 19
Small Crack D 128
Small Dreams E3 79
** Smash Your Glasses E5 64
Sneaking Sally Through the Alley VS 45
** Snug as a Thug on a Jug E4 133
* So Many Classics, So Little Time HVS 29
Sociology S 124
Soft Shoe VS 112
Sogines HVS 40
Solo Slab HVS 37
South Sea Charmer HVS 127
Space Junk HVS 118
Spare Rib VD 132
Spartacaid HVS 64
Spasticus Artisticus E3 120
Spearing the Bearded Clam E2 95
Spectacle S 32
Splinter HVS 62
Spock Out VS 27
Spring Sunshine VS 29
Spur Slab D 71
Squally Showers VS 80
Square Buttress Arête VS 130
Square Buttress Direct VS 129

Square Buttress Wall	S	130
Square Chimney	M	129
Stacked Blocks	VS	79
Stage Fright	E2	113
Staircase Rib	MD	37
Stairway Crack	Easy	36
* Stanage Without Oxygen	E5	131
** Stanleyville	E4	105
Star Trek	E5	82
Start	VS	19
Stealth	VS	73
Steamin'	HVS	20
Step-ladder Crack (direct)	HVS	103
** Step-ladder Crack	VS	103
Still in Limbo	E1	103
Stirrup	HS	71
Straight Ahead	D	87
Straight and Narrow	HVS	117
Straight Chimney	VD	116
Straight Crack	S	39
Straight Crack	VS	113
Straightsville	E2	117
* Strangler, The	E4	76
Straw Crack	S	89
* Stretcher Case	E2	75
Stretcher, The	VS	57
Stringer	HS	111
* Sudoxe	HVS	33
Suitored	E4	35
** Surgeon's Saunter	HVS	22
Surprise - Direct Start	E?	61
Surprise	HVS	61
* Suzanne	HVS	130
Swings	5c	100
Swooper	E5	76
Symbiosis	VS	87
Tales of Yankee Power	E1	63
* Tango Buttress	HS	41
Tango Crack	VD	41
Tarzan Boy	E3	97
Taurus Crack	HS	82
Tea-leaf Crack	VD	110
Tears and Guts	E2	63
Teenage Lobotomy	HVS	42
* Telli	E3	89
Tempskya	E3	28
Terrace Gully	VD	76
*** Terrazza Crack	HVS	27
Thalidomide	E2	32
That Sad Man	E2	118
Thrombosis	VS	107
* Thunder Road	E3	113
Tier Climb	VD	125
Time and Tide	VS	52
Timothy Twinkletoes	E3	35
Tinker's Crack	VS	124
Tip Off	E1	124
*** Tippler Direct	E3	121
*** Tippler, The	E1	121
** Titanic	VS	44
* Titanic Direct	HVS	44
Titbit	VS	111
Toggle	VS	129
* Tom-cat Slab	HVS	60
Too Cold to be Bold	E2	82
Toothcomb	VS	65
Top Block Rock	VD	97
Topaz	E4	115
** Torture Garden	E3	59
Touched	HVS	55
Tower Block	E3	93
* Tower Chimney	HVS	74
* Tower Crack	HVS	74
** Tower Face	HVS	75
Tower Face Direct	E2	75
* Tower Face Indirect	VS	75
Tower Gully	S	74
Tower Traverse	E1	75
* Townsend's Variation	HVS	120
Toxic	D	59
Trainer Failure	VS	131
Tram Eaters	E2	60
** Traverse of the Gritstone Gods	E4	134
Traversty	HVS	90
* Travesties	HVS	35
Treatment	VS	33
Trench Deadlock	HVS	53
Tribute to Kitty	E5	123
* Trickledown Fairy, The	E5	57
Tridymite Slab	VS	86
Trimming the Beard	E2	95
Trinket	S	100
Triplet	VS	108
Trivial Pursuit	S	128
True North	VS	132
Tumble Down	VS	93
Turf Crack	VD	100
Turnbull Missed	VS	87
Turnbull's Trajectory	S	86
Turnover	D	51
*** Turtle Power	E6	28
* Twin Cam	E4	131
** Twin Chimneys Buttress	VS	108
Twin Cracks	D	112
Twin Cracks	VD	24
Twinkle Toes	M	106
Twintrin	E1	115
* Twisting Crack	S	39
Twisting Crack Direct	-	39
Two Tier Climb	VD	125
Tying the Knot	E3	62
Typhoon	HS	36

Typhoon Direct	E3	36
Typical Grit	VD	42
*** Ulysses	E6	68
Undercut Crack	VS	31
Unleaded	S	72
Uno Crack	D	37
Unpredictable	HVS	83
** Unprintable, The	E1	121
Unthinkable, The	E2	94
Upanover	VS	106
Upanover Crack	S	106
Vaccine Traverse	E1	25
* Valediction	HVS	24
* Valhalla	VS	82
Vanishing Point	VS	101
Vanquished	E5	91
Velcro Arête	VD	129
* Vena Cave-in	E3	28
Ventured Point	HS	32
* Verandah Buttress	HVD	98
Verandah Cracks	D	99
* Verandah Pillar	HS	99
Verandah Wall	VS	99
Via Dexter	E2	116
Via Dexter Variation	HVS	116
* Via Media	VS	116
Via Roof Route	VS	108
* Vice, The	HVS	21
Video Nasty	E1	70
Vision Set	E1	90
Waffti	VD	61
Waiting for the Men In Black	HVS	52
Walking the Whippet	E3	83
Wall and Slab	VD	47
* Wall Buttress	VS	88
Wall End Crack	S	67
Wall End Flake Crack	VS	67
Wall End Girdle	VS	69
Wall End Holly Tree Crack	HS	68
** Wall End Slab	VS	65
* Wall End Slab Direct	E3	65
* Wall End Slab Super Duper Direct	E4	65
*** Wall of Sound	E5	114
Walrus Butter	E4	88
War Zone	HVS	125
Warlock	HVS	61
Warm Afternoon	VD	38
Warm September	VS	50
Watch-tower, The	HVS	93
Water Seller, The	E4	24
Waterloo Branch	HS	74
Wax Museum	HVS	102
Way Fruitsome Experience	HVS	39
Wearing Thin	E2	110
** Weather Report	E5	62
Wedge Gully	VS	119
Wedge Rib	VS	119
Wedge, The	VS	119
Well Right	E2	115
Wetness Wall	D	26
Whatever Happened to Bob?	E2	133
Where did my Tango?	VS	41
* Which Doctor?	E5	22
Whimper	HVD	63
*** White Wand	E5	69
Wing Buttress	VS	95
Wing Buttress Gully	D	95
Wing Wall	M	95
* Withered Thing	E2	110
* Wobbler, The	HVS	23
** Wolf Solent	E4	36
Wolf Solent Variant	E4	36
Wright's Route	VS	114
*** Wuthering	E2	109
X-ray	HS	34
Y Crack, The	VS	122
* Yosemite Wall	E2	117
You	VS	19
Youth	VD	38
Youth Meat	E4	36
Z Crack, The	VS	122
Zagrete	VS	113
Zel	VS	101
Zero Point	HVS	83
Zero Zero Sputnik	E1	61
Zip Crack	M	129
Zit	VS	51